THE
ARMY AND NAVY
PRAYER BOOK

OF THE

CONFEDERATE STATES
OF AMERICA

edited by

Dr. William G. Peters

CHATTANOOGA:
C. S. Printing Office
2014

Originally published in Richmond, Virginia, A.D. 1865,

by the

𝕯𝖎𝖔𝖈𝖊𝖘𝖆𝖓 𝕸𝖎𝖘𝖘𝖎𝖔𝖓𝖆𝖗𝖞 𝕾𝖔𝖈𝖎𝖊𝖙𝖞

of the Protestant Episcopal Church
of Virginia, in the

CONFEDERATE STATES OF AMERICA.

Published by the CONFEDERATE STATES PRINTING OFFICE[1], CONFEDERATE STATES OF AMERICA, INC.

---

[1] A division of the Confederate States of America, Inc. Also designated the C.S. PRINTING OFFICE.

CONTENTS

FOREWORD

The Army Navy Prayer Book was produced by the Protestant Episcopal Church in the Confederate States of America for the benefit of the military forces of the Confederacy.

The Episcopal dioceses in the South began to change their allegiance from the "Protestant Episcopal Church in the United States of America" as their States became a part of the C.S.A.

The first diocese to leave the PECUSA was that of Louisiana, whose bishop, Leonidas Polk, issued a proclamation on 30 January 1861, stating:

"The State of Louisiana having, by a formal ordinance, through her Delegates in Convention assembled, withdrawn herself from all further connection with the United States of America, and constituted herself a separate Sovereignty, has, by that act, removed our Diocese from within the pale of 'The Protestant Episcopal Church in the United States.'"

It goes on to state:

"Our separation from our brethren of The Protestant Episcopal Church in the United States has been effected because we must follow our nationality. Not because there has been any difference of opinion as to Christian Doctrine or Catholic usage."

Thereafter, the Church became the Protestant Episcopal Church in the Confederate States, under the governance of its bishops in the Confederacy.

Bp. Leonidas Polk was commissioned a General in the Army of the Confederate States, and fought as a corps commander in many of the battles in the Western theater.

He was an 1827 graduate of West Point, a leading founder of the University of the South, which he envisioned as a national university of the South. Bp. Polk earned the epithet, The Fighting Bishop, and was killed on 14 June 1864 at Pine Mountain, Georgia, while scouting out enemy positions.

The Army Navy Prayer Book went through several editions, ending with the 1865 edition.

As an Afterword, some additional prayers by Bp. Thomas Atkinson, bishop of North Carolina, have been included. Also added are national calls to prayer by President Jefferson Davis, and a sermon by Bp. Stephen Elliot delivered upon the Day of National Humiliation, Fasting and Prayer in 1861.

In the present day struggle for survival of Christian religion and Confederate culture, we must not forget that while we must work as if everything depends upon us, we must pray for everything depends on God's grace and blessing.

Prayer and devotions were much a part of the Confederate Army, for it considered itself above all, a *Christian* Army.

The South remains the bastion of the Christian Faith upon the American continent.

This Army Navy Prayer Book is reprinted as a resource for Confederate citizens under our continuing occupation by Yankee government.

DEO VINDICE!

Dr. William G. Peters
President
THE CONFEDERATE STATES OF AMERICA, INC.
Anno Domini 2014

THE ORDER FOR
MORNING PRAYER

¶ *The Minister shall begin by reading one or more of the following Sentences of Scripture:*

THE LORD is in his holy temple; let all the earth keep silence before him. *Hab.* 2:20.

When the wicked man turneth away from his wickedness that he hath committed, and doeth that which is lawful and right, he shall save his soul alive. *Ezek.* 18:27.

The sacrifices of God are a broken spirit; a broken and a contrite heart, O God, thou wilt not despise. *Psalm* 51:17.

Rend your heart, and not your garments, and turn unto the LORD your God; for he is gracious and merciful, slow to anger, and of great kindness, and repenteth him of the evil. *Joel* 2:19.

I will arise and go to my father, and will say unto him, Father, I have sinned against heaven, and before thee, and am no more worthy to be called thy son. *St. Luke 15:18-19.*

Enter not into judgment with thy servant, O LORD; for in thy sight shall no man living be justified. *Psalm 112:2.*

If we say that we have no sin, we deceive ourselves, and the truth is not in us; but if we confess our sin, God is faithful and just to forgive us our sins, and to cleanse us from all unrighteousness. *1 John 1:8-9.*

¶ *Then the Minister shall say,*

DEARLY beloved brethren, the Scripture moveth us in sundry places, to acknowledge and confess our manifold bins and wickedness; and that we should not dissemble nor cloak them before the face of Almighty God our heavenly father; but confess them with an humble, lowly, penitent and obedient heart; to the end that we may obtain forgiveness of the same, by his infinite goodness and mercy. And although we ought, at all times, humbly to acknowledge our sins before God; yet ought we chiefly so to do, when we assemble and meet together to render thanks for the great benefits that we have received at his hands, to set forth his most worthy praise, to hear his most holy Word, and to ask those things which are requisite and necessary, as well for the body as the soul. Wherefore I pray and beseech you, as many as are here present, to accompany me with a pure heart, and humble voice, unto the throne of the heavenly grace, saying,

A General Confession

¶ *To be said by the whole Congregation, after the Minister, all kneeling.*

ALMIGHTY and most merciful Father; we have erred, and strayed from thy ways like lost sheep. We have followed too much the devices and desires of our own hearts. We have offended against thy holy laws. We have left undone those things which we ought to have done; And we have done those things which we ought not to have done; And there is no health in us. But thou, O Lord, have merely upon us, miserable offenders. Spare thou those, O God, who confess their faults. Restore thou those who are penitent; According to thy promiser O s declared unto mankind in Christ Jesus our Lord. And grant, O most merciful Father, for his sake: That we may hereafter live a godly, righteous, and sober life, To the glory of thy holy Name. Amen.

The Declaration of Absolution, or Remission of Sins.

¶ *The people shall answer here, and at the end of every Prayer, Amen.*

ALMIGHTY God, our heavenly Father, who of his great mercy hath promised forgiveness of sins to all those, who with hearty repentance and true faith, turn not him; Have mercy upon you; pardon and liver you from all your sins, confirm and strengthen you in all goodness; and bring you to everlasting life; through Jesus Christ our Lord. Amen.

¶ *Then the Minister shall kneel, and say the Lord's Prayer; the People still kneeling, and repeating it with him.*

OUR Father, who art in heaven, Hallowed   be thy name. Thy Kingdom come. Thy will be done on earth, As it is in heaven. Give us this day our daily bread. And forgive us our trespasses, As We forgive those who trespass against us. And lead us not into temptation; But deliver us from evil; For thine is the kingdom, and the power, and the glory, for ever and ever. Amen.

¶ Then likewise he shall say,

O Lord, open thou our lips.

Answer. And our mouth shall show forth thy praise.

¶ Here, all standing up, the Minister shall say,

Glory be to the Father, and to the Son, and to the Holy Ghost;

Answer. As it was in the beginning, is now, and ever shall be, world without end.

Minister. Praise ye the Lord.

Answer. The Lord's Name be praised.

¶ then shall be said or sung the following Anthem:

Venite, exultemus Domino.

O COME, let us sing unto the LORD; let us heartily rejoice in the strength of our salvation.

Let us come before his presence with thanksgiving; and show ourselves glad in him with psalms.

For the LORD is a great God; and a great king above all gods.

In his hand are all the corners of the earth; and the strength of the hills is his also.

The sea is his, and he made it; and his hands prepared the dry land.

O come let us worship and fall down, and kneel before the LORD our Maker.

For he is the LORD our God; and we are the people of his pasture, and the sheep of his hand.

O worship the LORD in the beauty of holiness; let the whole earth stand in awe of him.

For he cometh, for he cometh to judge the earth; and with righteousness to judge the world, and the people with his truth.

SELECTIONS.
No. 1.

Then shall be read one of the following Selections — Minister and People reading alternate verses:

Psalm 51. From S. III.

H AVE mercy upon me, O God, after thy great goodness; according to the multitude of thy mercies do away mine offences.

Wash me thoroughly from my wickedness, and cleanse me from my sins,

For I acknowledge my faults, and my sin is ever before me.

Against thee only have I sinned, and done this evil in thy sight; that thou mightest be justified in thy saying, and clear when thou art judged.

Behold, I was shapen in wickedness, and in sin hath my mother conceived me.

But lo thou requirest truth in the inward parts, and shalt make me to understand wisdom secretly.

Thou shalt purge me with hyssop, and I shall be clean; thou shalt wash me, and I shall be whiter than snow.

Thou shalt make me hear of joy and gladness, that the bones which thou hast broken may rejoice.

Turn thy face from my sins, and put out all my misdeeds.

Make, me a clean heart, O God, and renew a right spirit within me.

Cast me not away from thy presence, and take not thy Holy Spirit from me.

O give me the comfort of thy help again, and stablish me with thy free Spirit.

Then shall I teach thy ways unto the wicked, and sinners shall be converted unto thee.

Deliver me from blood guiltiness, O God, thou that art the God of my health; and my tongue shall sing of thy righteousness.

Thou shalt open my lips, O Lord, and my mouth shall show thy praise.

For thou desirest no sacrifice, else would I give it thee; but thou delightest not in burnt-offerings.

The sacrifice of God is a troubled spirit: a broken and contrite heart, O God, shalt thou not despise.

From Psalm 42. *Quemadmodum.*

LIKE as the hart desireth the water brooks, so longeth my soul after thee, O God.

My soul is athirst for God, yea, even for the living God; when shall I come to appear before the presence of God?

My tears have been my meat day and night, while they daily say unto me, Where is now thy God?

Now when I think thereupon, I pour out my heart by myself; for I went with the multitude, and brought them forth into the house of God;

In the voice of praise and thanksgiving, among such as keep holyday.

Why art thou so full of heaviness, O my soul, and why art thou so disquieted within me?

Put thy trust in God; for I will yet give him thanks for the help of his countenance.

The LORD hath granted his loving kindness in the daytime; and in the night-season did I sing of him, and made my prayer unto the God of my life.

I will say unto the God of my strength, Why hast thou forgotten me? why go I thus heavily, while the enemy oppresseth me?

Namely, while they say daily unto me, Where is now thy God?

Why art than so vexed, O my soul? and why art thou so disquieted within me?

O put thy trust in God; for I will yet thank him, which is the help of my countenance and my God.

No. 2.

Psalm 32. From S. VI.

BLESSED is he whose unrighteousness is   forgiven, and whose sin is covered.

Blessed is the man unto whom the LORD imputeth no sin, and in whose spirit there is no guile.

I will acknowledge my sin unto thee; and mine unrighteousness have I not hid.

I said, I will confess my sins unto the LORD; and so thou forgavest the wickedness of my sin.

For this shall every one that is godly make his prayer unto thee, in a time when thou mayest be found; but in the great water-floods they shall not come nigh him.

Thou art a place to hide me in; thou shalt preserve me from trouble; thou shalt compass me about with songs of deliverance.

I will inform thee, and teach thee in the way wherein thou shalt go; and I will guide thee with mine eye.

Great plagues remain for the ungodly; but whoso putteth his trust in the LORD, mercy embraceth him on every side.

Be glad, O ye righteous, and rejoice in the LORD; and be joyful, all ye that are true of heart.

Psalm 70.

OUT of the deep have I called unto thee, O LORD; LORD, hear my voice.

O let thine eyes consider well the voice of my complaint.

If thou, LORD, wilt be extreme to mark what is done amiss, O LORD, who may abide it?

For there is mercy with thee; therefore shalt thou be feared.

I look for the LORD; my soul doth wait for him; in his word is my trust.

My soul fleeth unto the LORD before the morning watch; I say, before the Morning watch.

O Israel, trust in the LORD; for with the LORD there is mercy, and with him is plenteous redemption.

And he shall redeem Israel from all his sins.

Psalm 121.

I WILL lift up mine eyes unto the hills, from whence cometh my help.

My help cometh even from the LORD, who hath made heaven and earth.

He will not suffer thy foot to be moved; and he that keepeth thee will not sleep.

Behold, he that keepeth Israel shall neither slumber nor sleep.

The LORD himself is thy keeper; the LORD is thy defense upon thy right hand;

So that the sun shall not burn thee by day; neither the moon by night.

The LORD shall preserve thee from all evil; yea, it is even he that shall keep thy soul.

The LORD shall preserve thy going out and thy coming in, from this time forth fur ever-more.

No. 3.   S. VII.

Psalm 23. Dominus regit me.

THE LORD is my shepherd; therefore can I lack nothing. He shall feed me in a green pasture, and lead me forth beside the waters of comfort.

He shall convert my soul, and bring me forth in the paths of righteousness for his Name's sake.

Yea, though I walk through the valley of the shadow of death, I will fear no evil; for thou art with me; thy rod and thy staff comfort me. Thou shalt prepare a table before me against them that trouble me; thou hast anointed my head with oil, and my cup shall be full.

But thy loving kindness and mercy shall follow me all the days of my life; and I dwell in the house of the LORD forever.

Psalm 34. Benedicam Domino.

I WILL always give thanks unto the LORD, his praise shall ever be in my mouth.

My soul shall make her boast in the LORD; the humble shall hear thereof, and be glad.

O praise the LORD with me; and let us magnify his Name together.

I sought the LORD and he heard me; yea, he delivered me out of all my fear.

They had an eye unto him, and were lightened; and their faces were not ashamed.

Lo, the poor crieth, and the LORD heareth him; yea, and saveth him out of all his troubles.

The angel of the LORD tarrieth round about them that fear him, and delivereth them.

O taste, and see, how gracious the LORD is: blessed is the man that trusteth in him.

O fear the LORD, ye that are his saints; for they that fear him lack nothing.

The lions do lack and suffer hunger; but they who love the LORD shall want no manner of thing that is good.

Come, ye children, and hearken unto me: I will teach you the fear of the LORD.

What man is he that lusteth to live, and would fain see good days?

Keep thy tongue from evil, and thy lips, that they speak no guile.

Eschew evil, and do good; seek peace, and ensue it.

The eyes of the LORD are over the righteous, and his ears are open unto their prayers.

The countenance of the LORD is against them that do evil, to root out the remembrance of them front the earth.

The righteous cry, and the LORD heareth them, and delivereth them out of all their troubles.

Here may be said or sung the following Hymn:
Gloria in excelsis.

GLORY be to God on high, and on earth peace, good will towards men. We praise thee, we bless thee, we worship thee, we glorify thee, we give thanks to thee for by great glory, O LORD God, heavenly King, God the Father Almighty.

O LORD, the only-begotten Son Jesus Christ; O LORD God, Lamb of God, Son of the Father, that takest away the sins of the world, have mercy upon us. Thou that takest away the sins of the world, have mercy upon us. Thou that takest away the sins of the world, receive our prayer. Thou that sittest at the right hand of God the Father, have mercy upon us.

For thou only art holy; thou only art the Lord; thou only, O Christ, with the Holy Ghost art most high in the glory of God the Father. Amen.

Then shall be read the First Lesson—after which shall be said or sung the following Hymn:
Te Deum Laudamus.

W E praise thee, O God; we acknowledge thee to be the LORD. All the earth doth worship thee, the Father everlasting.

To thee all Angels cry aloud; the Heavens, and all the Powers therein.

To thee Cherubim, and Seraphim continually do cry, Holy, Holy, Holy, Lord God of Sabaoth;

Heaven and earth are full of the Majesty of thy Glory.

The glorious company of the Apostles praise thee.

The godly fellowship of the Prophets praise thee.

The noble army of Martyrs praise thee:

The holy Church throughout all the world doth acknowledge thee;

The Father, of an infinite Majesty;

Thine adorable, true, and only Son;

Also the Holy Ghost, the Comforter.

Thou art the King of Glory, O Christ.

Thou art the everlasting Son of the Father.

When thou tookest upon thee to deliver man, thou didst humble thyself to be born of a Virgin.

When thou hadst overcome the sharpness of death, thou didst open the Kingdom of Heaven to all believers.

Thou sittest at the right hand of God, in the Glory of the Father.

We believe that thou shalt come to be our Judge.

We therefore pray thee, help thy servants, whom thou hast redeemed with thy precious blood.

Make them to be numbered with thy Saints, in glory everlasting.

O Lord, save thy people, and bless thine heritage.

Govern them and lift them up for ever. Day by day we magnify thee;

And we worship, thy Name ever, world without end.

Vouchsafe, O LORD, to keep us this day without sin.

O LORD, have mercy upon us, have mercy upon us.

O LORD, let thy mercy be upon us, as our trust is in thee.

O LORD, in thee have I trusted; let me never be confounded.

¶ *Then shall be read the Second Lesson — after which the following Psalm may be said or sung:*

Psalm 100.

O BE joyful in the LORD, all ye lands: serve the Lord with gladness, and come before his presence with a song.

2 Be ye sure that the LORD he is God; it is he that hath made us, and not we ourselves; we are his people, and the sheep of his pasture.

3 O go your way into his gates with thanksgiving and into his courts with praise; be thankful unto him, and speak good of his Name.

4 For the LORD is gracious, his mercy is everlasting; and his truth endureth from generation to generation.

¶ *Then shall be said the Apostles' Creed, by their Minister and the People, standing.*

I BELIEVE in God the Father Almighty, Maker of heaven and earth:

And in Jesus Christ his only Son our Lord: Who was conceived by the Holy Ghost, Born of the Virgin Mary; Suffered under Pontius Pilate, Was crucified, dead, and buried; He descended into Hell, The third day he rose from the dead; He ascended into heaven, And sitteth on the right hand of God the Father Almighty; from thence he shall come to judge the quick and the dead.

I believe in the Holy Ghost; The holy Catholic Church, The Communion of Saints; The forgiveness of sins; The Resurrection of the body; And the Life everlasting. Amen.

¶ *And after that, these prayers following, all devoutly. kneeling; the Minister first pronouncing,*

The Lord be with you

Answer. And with thy spirit.

Minister. Let us pray.

O Lord, show thy mercy upon us.

Answer. And grant us thy salvation.

Minister. O God, make clean our hearts within us.

Answer. And take not thy Holy Spirit from us:

A Collect for Peace.

O GOD, who art the author of peace and lover of concord, in knowledge of whom standeth our eternal life, whose service is perfect freedom; Defend us; thy humble servants, in all assaults of our enemies; that we, surely trusting in thy defense, may not fear the power of any adversaries, through the might of Jesus Christ our Lord. *Amen.*

A Collect for Grace.

O LORD, our heavenly Father, Almighty and everlasting God, who hest safely brought: us to the beginning of this day; Defend as in the same with thy mighty power.; and grant that this day we fall into no sin, neither run into any kind of danger; but that all our doings, being ordered by thy governance, may be righteous in thy sight; through Jesus Christ our Lord. *Amen.*

A Prayer for **THE PRESIDENT OF THE CONFEDERATE STATES,**
and all in civil Authority.

O LORD, our heavenly Father, the high and mighty Ruler of
the universe, who dost from the throne behold all the
dwellers upon earth; Most heartily we beseech thee with thy
favor to behold and bless thy servant, **THE PRESIDENT OF
THE CONFEDERATE STATES,** and all others in authority; and
so replenish them with the grace of thy Holy Spirit, that
they may always incline to thy will, and walk in thy way.
Endue them plenteously with heavenly gifts; grant them in
health and prosperity long to live; and finally, after this life,
to attain everlasting joy and felicity; through Jesus Christ our
Lord. *Amen.*

A Prayer for the Clergy and People.

A LMIGHTY and everlasting God, from whom cometh
every good and perfect gift; Send down upon our
bishops, and other Clergy, and upon the Congregations
committed to their charge, the healthful spirit of thy grace;
and, that they may truly please thee, pour upon them the
continual dew of thy blessing. Grant this O Lord, for the
honor of our Advocate and Mediator Jesus Christ.

A Prayer for all Conditions of Men.

O GOD, the Creator and Preserver of all mankind, we
humbly beseech thee for all sorts and conditions of men;
that thou Wouldst be pleased to make thy ways known unto
them, thy saving health unto all nations. More- especially we
pray for thy holy Church universal; that it may be so guided
and governed by thy good Spirit, that all who profess and
call themselves Christian may be led into the way of truth,
and hold the faith in unity of spirit, in the bond of peace,
and in righteousness of life. Finally, we commend to thy
fatherly goodness all those who are in any ways afflicted, or
distressed, in mind, body, or estate; that it may please thee to
comfort and relieve them according to their several
necessities giving them patience under their sufferings and a
happy issue out of all their affliction's. And this we beg for
Jesus Christ's sake. *Amen.*

A General Thanksgiving.

A LMIGHTY God, Father of all mercies, we, thine
unworthy servants, do give thee most humble and hearty

thanks for all thy goodness and loving-kindness to us, and to all men. We bless thee for our creation, preservation, and all the blessings of this life; but above all, for thine inestimable love in the redemption of the world by our Lord Jesus Christ; for the means of grace, and for the hope of glory. And we beseech thee, give us that due sense of all thy mercies, that our hearts may be unfeignedly thankful, and that we may show forth thy praise, not only with our lips, but in our lives; by giving up ourselves to thy service, and by walking before thee in holiness and righteousness all our days; through Jesus Christ. our Lord, to whom, with thee and the Holy Ghost, be all honor and glory, world without end. *Amen.*

A Prayer of St. Chrysostom.

ALMIGHTY God, who hast given us grace at this time with one accord to make our common supplications unto thee; and dost promise that when two or three are gathered together in thy Name thou wilt grant their requests; Fulfill now, O Lord, the desires and petitions of thy servants, as may be most expedient for them; granting us in this world knowledge of thy truth, and in the world to come life everlasting. *Amen.*

2 Cor. 13:14.

THE grace of our Lord Jesus Christ, and the love of God, and the fellowship of the Holy Ghost, be with us all evermore. Amen.

A SECOND SERVICE.

The Minister shall begin by reading the following Sentences:

L ET the words of my mouth, and the meditation of my heart be always acceptable in thy sight, O LORD, my strength and my Redeemer. *Ps.* 19:14-15.

When the wicked man turneth away from his wickedness that he hath committed, and doeth that which is lawful and right, he shall save his soul alive. *Ezek.* 18:27.

¶ Then the Minister shall say,

D EARLY beloved brethren, I pray and beseech you, as many as are here present, to accompany me with a pure heart, and humble voice, unto the throne of the heavenly grace.

THE LITANY,
OR GENERAL SUPPLICATION.

(To be said by the Minister and People alternately, all kneeling.)

O God the Father of Heaven; have mercy upon us miserable sinners.

O God the Father of Heaven; have mercy upon us miserable sinners.

O God the Son, Redeemer of the world; have mercy upon us miserable sinners.

O God the Son, Redeemer of the world; have mercy upon us miserable sinners.

O God the Holy Ghost, proceeding from the Father and the Son;. have mercy upon us miserable sinners.

O God the Holy Ghost, proceeding from the Father and the Son; have mercy upon us miserable sinners.

O holy, blessed, and glorious Trinity, three Persons and one God; have mercy upon us miserable sinners.

O holy, blessed, and, glorious Trinity, three Persons and one God; have mercy upon us miserable sinners.

Remember not, Lord, our offences, nor the offences of our forefathers; neither take thou vengeance of our sins; spare us, good Lord, spare thy people, whom thou hast redeemed with thy most precious blood, and be not angry with us for ever.

Spare us, good Lord.

From all evil and mischief; from sin; from the crafts and assaults of the devil; from thy wrath, and from everlasting damnation,

Good Lord, deliver us.

From all blindness of heart; from pride, vain-glory, and hypocrisy; from envy, hatred, and malice, and all uncharitableness,

Good Lord, deliver us.

From all inordinate and sinful affections and from all the deceits of the world, the flesh, and the devil.

Good Lord, deliver us.

From lightning and tempest; from plague, pestilence, and famine; from battle and murder, and from sudden death,

Good Lord, deliver us.

From all sedition, privy conspiracy, and rebellion; from all false doctrine, heresy, and schism; from hardness of heart, and contempt of thy Word and Commandment,

Good Lord, deliver us.

By the mystery of thy holy Incarnation; by thy holy Nativity and Circumcision; by thy Baptism, Fasting, and Temptation,

Good Lord, deliver us.

By thine Agony and Bloody Sweat; by thy Cross and Passion; by thy precious Death and Burial; by thy glorious Resurrection and Ascension; and by the coming of the Holy Ghost.

Good Lord, deliver us.

In all time of our tribulation; in all time of our prosperity; in the hour of death, and in the day of judgment,

Good Lord, deliver us.

We sinners do beseech thee to hear us, O LORD God; and that it may please thee to rule and govern thy holy Church universal in the right way;

We beseech thee to hear us, good Lord.

That it may please thee to bless and preserve all Christian Rulers and Magistrates; giving them grace to execute justice, and to maintain truth;

We beseech thee to hear us, good Lord.

That it may please thee to illuminate all Bishops, Priests, and Deacons, with true knowledge and understanding of thy Word; and that both by their preaching and living they may set it forth, and show it accordingly;

We beseech thee to hear us, good Lord.

That it may please thee to bless and keep all thy people;

We beseech thee to hear us, good Lord.

That it may please thee to give to all nations unity, peace, and concord;

We beseech thee to hear us, good Lord.

That it may please thee to give us an heart to love and fear thee, and diligently to live after thy commandments;

We beseech thee to hear us, good Lord.

That it may please thee to give to all thy people increase of grace to hear meekly thy Wore, and to receive it with pure affection, and to bring forth the fruits of the Spirit;

We beseech thee to hear us, good Lord.

That it may please thee to bring into the way of truth all such as have erred, and are deceived;

We beseech thee to hear us, good Lord.

That it may please thee to strengthen such as do stand; and to comfort and help the weak-hearted and to raise up those who fall; and finally to beat down, Satan under our feet;

We beseech thee to hear us, good Lord.

That it may please thee to succor, help, and comfort all who are in danger, necessity, and tribulation;

We beseech thee to hear us, good Lord.

That it may please thee to preserve all who travel by land or by water, all women in the perils of child-birth, all sick persons and young children: and to show thy pity upon all prisoners and captives;

We beseech thee to hear us, good Lord.

That it may please thee to defend, and provide for, the fatherless children, and widows, and all who are desolate and oppressed;

We beseech thee to hear us, good Lord.

That it may please thee to have mercy upon all men;

We beseech thee to hear us, good Lord.

That it may please thee to forgive our enemies, persecutors, and slanderers, and to turn their hearts;

We beseech thee to hear us, good Lord.

That it may please thee to give and preserve to our use the kindly fruits of the earth, o that in due time we may enjoy them;

We beseech thee to hear us, good Lord.

That it may please thee to give us true repentance; to forgive us all our sins, negligences and ignorances; and to endue us with the grace of thy Holy Spirit to amend our lives according to thy Holy Word;

We beseech thee to hear us, good Lord.

Son of God, we beseech thee to hear us.

Son of God, we beseech thee to hear us.

O Lamb of God, who takest away the sins of the world;

Grant us thy peace.

O Lamb of God, who takest away the sins of the world;

Have mercy upon us.

¶ *The Minister may, at his discretion, omit all that follows, to the Prayer, "We humbly beseech thee, O Father," &c.*

O Christ, hear us.

O Christ, hear us.

Lord, have mercy upon us.

Lord, have mercy upon us.

Christ, have mercy upon us.

Christ, have mercy upon us.

Lord, have mercy upon us.

Lord, have mercy upon us.

¶ *Then shall the Minister, and the People with him, say the Lord's Prayer.*

OUR Father, who art in heaven, Hallowed be thy Name. Thy kingdom come. Thy will be done on earth, As it is in heaven.

Give us this day our daily bread. And forgive us our trespasses, As we forgive those who trespass against us. And lead us not into temptation; But deliver us from evil. Amen.

Minister. O Lord, deal not with us according our sins.

Answer. Neither reward us according to our iniquities.

Let us pray.

O GOD, merciful Father, who despisest not the sighing of a contrite heart, nor the desire of such as are sorrowful; Mercifully assist our prayers which we make before thee in all our troubles and adversities, whensoever they oppress. us; and graciously hear us, that those evils which the craft and subtlety of the devil or man worketh against us, May, by thy good providence, be brought to naught; that we thy servants, being hurt by no persecutions, may evermore give thanks unto thee in thy holy Church; through Jesus Christ our Lord.

O Lord, arise, help us, and deliver us for thy Name's sake.

O GOD, we have heard with our ears, and our fathers have declared unto us, the noble works that thou didst in their days, and in the old time before them.

O LORD, arise, help us, and deliver us for thine honor.

Glory be to the Father, and to the Son and to the Holy Ghost;

Answer. As it was in the beginning, now, and ever shall be, world without end. Amen.

From our enemies defend us, O Christ.

Graciously look upon our afflictions.

With pity behold the sorrows of our hearts

Mercifully forgive the sins of thy people

Favorably with mercy hear our prayers.

O Son of David, have mercy upon us.

Both now and ever vouchsafe to hear us O Christ.

Graciously hear us, O Christ; graciously, hear us, O Lord Christ.

Minister. O Lord, let thy mercy be showed upon us;

Answer. As we do put our trust in thee.

Let us pray.

WE humbly beseech thee, O Father, mercifully to look upon our infirmities; and, for the glory of thy Name; turn from us all those evils that we most justly have deserved; and grant, that in all our troubles we may put our whole trust and confidence in thy mercy, and evermore serve thee in holiness and pureness of living, to thy honor I and glory; through our only Mediator and Advocate, Jesus Christ our Lord. *Amen.*

A General Thanksgiving.

ALMIGHTY God, Father of all mercies, we, thine unworthy servants, do give thee most humble and hearty thanks for all thy goodness and loving-kindness to us, and to all men. We bless thee for our creation, preservation, and all the blessings of this life; but above all, for thine inestimable love in the redemption of the world by our Lord Jesus Christ; for the means of grace, and for the hope of glory. And, we beseech thee, give us that due sense of all thy mercies, that our hearts may be unfeignedly thankful; and that we may show forth thy praise, not only with our lips, but in our lives; by giving up ourselves to thy service, and by walking before thee in holiness and righteousness all our days; through Jesus Christ our Lord, to whom, with thee and the Holy Ghost, be all honor and glory, world without end. *Amen.*

A Prayer of St. Chrysostom.

ALMIGHTY God, who hast given us grace at this time with one accord to make our common supplications unto thee; and dost promise that when two or three are gathered together in thy Name, thou wilt grant their requests; Fulfill now, O Lord, the desires and petitions of thy servants, as may be most expedient for them; granting us in this world knowledge of thy truth, and in the world to t come life everlasting. *Amen.*

2 Cor. 13:14.

THE grace of our Lord Jesus Christ, and the love of God, and the fellowship of the Holy Ghost, be with us all evermore. Amen.

A THIRD SERVICE.

H IDE thy face from my sins; and blot out all mine iniquities. *Psalm* 51:17.

The sacrifices of God are a broken spirit; a broken and a contrite heart, O God, thou wilt not despise. *Psalm* li. 17.

¶ Then the Minister shall say,

D EARLY beloved brethren, i pray and beseech you, as many as are here present, to accompany me with a pure heart, an humble voice, unto the throne of the heavenly grace.

A General Confession.

¶ To be said by the whole Congregation, after the Minister, all kneeling.

A LMIGHTY and most merciful Father; we have erred and strayed from the ways like lost sheep. We have followed too much the devices and desires of our own hearts. We have offended against thy holy laws. We have left undone those things, which we ought to have done; And we have done those things which we ought not to have done; and there is no health in us. But thou, O Lord, have mercy upon us, miserable offenders. Spare thou those, O God, who confess their faults. Restore thou those who are penitent; According to thy promises declared unto mankind in Christ Jesus our Lord. And grant, O most merciful Father, for his sake; That we may hereafter live a godly, righteous, and sober life; To the glory of thy holy Name. Amen.

The Declaration of Absolution or Remission of Sins.

A LMIGHTY God, our heavenly Father, who of his great mercy hath promised forgiveness of sins to all those, who with hearty repentance and true faith, turn unto him; Have mercy upon you; pardon and deliver you from all your sins, confirm and strengthen you in all goodness; and bring you to everlasting life; through Jesus Christ our Lord. *Amen.*

O UR Father, who art in heaven, Hallowed be thy Name. Thy kingdom come. Thy be done on earth, As it is in heaven.

Give us this day our daily bread. And forgive us our trespasses, As we forgive those who trespass against us. And lead us not into temptation; But deliver .us from evil; For thine is the kingdom, and the power, and the glory, for ever and ever. *Amen.*

The Collect.

A LMIGHTY God, unto whom all hearts   are open, all desires known, and from whom no secrets are hid: Cleanse the thoughts of our hearts by the inspiration of thy Holy Spirit, that we may perfectly love thee, and worthily magnify thy holy Name; through Christ our Lord. *Amen.*

¶ Then shall the Minister turning to the People, rehearse distinctly the **TEN COMMANDMENTS;** and the People, still kneeling, shall, after every Commandment, ask God's mercy for their transgressions for the time past, and grace to keep the law far the time to come, as followeth:

Minister.

G OD spake these words, and said: I am I the Lord thy God; Thou shalt have none other gods but me.

People. Lord, have mercy upon us, and incline our hearts to keep this law.

Minister. Thou shalt not make to thyself any graven image, nor the likeness of an thing that is in heaven above, or in the earth beneath; or in the water under the earth. Thou shalt not bow down to them, nor worship them: for I the Lord thy God am a jealous God, and visit the sins of the fathers upon the children, unto the third and fourth generation of them that hate me; and show mercy unto thousands in them that love me, and keep, my commandments.

People Lord, have mercy upon us, and incline our hearts to keep this law.

Minister: Thou shalt not take the Name of the Lord, thy God in vain: for the Lord will not hold him guiltless, that taketh his Name in vain.

People. Lord, have mercy upon us, and incline our hearts to keep this law.

Minister. Remember. that thou keep holy the Sabbath day. Six days shalt thou labor, and do all that thou hast to do; but the seventh day is the Sabbath of the Lord thy God. In it thou shalt do no manner of work; thou, and thy son, and thy daughter, thy man-servant, and thy maid servant, thy cattle, and, the stranger that is within thy gates. For in six days the Lord made heaven and earth, sea, and all that in them is, and rested the seventh day; wherefore the Lord blessed the seventh day, and hallowed it.

People. Lord, have mercy upon us, and incline our hearts to keep this law.

Minister. Honor thy father and thy mother; that thy days may be long in the land which the Lord thy God giveth thee.

People. Lord, have mercy upon us, and incline our hearts to keep this law.

Minister. Thou shalt do no murder.

People. Lord, have mercy upon us, and incline our hearts to keep this law.

Minister. Thou shalt not commit adultery:

People. Lord, have mercy upon us, and incline our hearts to keep this law.

Minister. Thou shalt not steal.

People. Lord, have mercy upon us, and incline our hearts to keep this law.

Minister. Thou shalt not bear false witness against thy neighbor.

People. Lord, have mercy upon us, and incline our hearts to keep this law.

Minister. Thou shalt not covet thy neighbor's house, thou shalt not covet thy neighbor's wife, nor his servant, nor his maid, nor his ox, nor his ass, nor any thing that is his.

People. Lord, have mercy upon us, and write all these thy laws in our hearts, we beseech thee.

Then the Minister may say:

Hear also what our Lord Jesus Christ sayeth.

THOU shalt love the Lord thy God, with all thy heart, and with all thy soul, and with all thy mind. This is the first and great commandment. And the second is like unto it: Thou shalt love thy neighbor as thyself. On these two commandments hang all the Law and the Prophets.

Let us pray.

O ALMIGHTY Lord, and everlasting God, vouchsafe, we beseech thee, to direct, sanctify, and govern, both our hearts and bodies, in the ways of thy laws, and in the works of thy commandments; that, through thy most mighty, protection, both here and ever, we may be preserved in body and soul; I through Our Lord and Saviour Jesus Christ. *Amen.*

2 Cor. 13:14.

THE grace of our Lord Jesus Christ, and the love of God, and the fellowship of the Holy Ghost, be with us all evermore.

OCCASIONAL PRAYERS.

B LESSED Lord, who hast caused all holy Scriptures to be written for our learning; Grant that we may in such wise hear them, lead, mark, learn, and inwardly digest them, that by patience, and comfort of Thy Holy Word, we may embrace, and ever hold fast the blessed hope of everlasting life, which Thou hast given us in our Saviour Jesus Christ. Amen.

A LMIGHTY God, Father of our Lord Jesus Christ, Maker of all things, Judge of all men; We acknowledge and bewail our manifold sins and wickedness, Which we from time to time, most grievously have committed; by thought, word and deed, Against; Thy Divine Majesty, Provoking most justly Thy wrath. and indignation against us. We, do earnestly repent, And are heartily sorry for these our misdoings; The remembrance of them is grievous unto us; The burden of them is intolerable. Have mercy upon us,

Have mercy upon us, most merciful Father; For thy Son our Lord Jesus Christ's sake, forgive us all that is past; And grant that we may ever hereafter Serve and please Thee in newness of life, To the honor and glory of Thy name; through Jesus Christ our Lord. Amen.

O MOST mighty God and merciful Father, who hast compassion open all men, and hatest nothing that thou hast made; who wouldest not the death of a sinner; but rather that he should turn from his sin,, and be saved; Mercifully forgive us our trespasses receive and comfort us, who are grieved and wearied with the burden of our sins. Thy property is always to have mercy; to Thee only it appertaineth to forgive sins. Spare us, therefore, good Lord, spare thy people, whom thou hast redeemed; enter not into judgment with thy servants, who are vile earth, and miserable sinners; but so turn thy anger from us, who meekly acknowledge our vileness, and truly repent us of our faults, and so make haste to help us in this world, that we may ever live with thee in the world to come; through Jesus Christ our Lord. Amen.

For Persons under Affliction.

O MERCIFUL God, and heavenly Father, who hast taught us in Thy Holy Word that Thou dost not willingly afflict or grieve the children of men; Look with pity, we beseech Thee, upon the sorrows of Thy servants, for whom our prayers are desired. In Thy wisdom, Thou hast seen fit to visit them with trouble; and to bring distress upon them. Remember them, O Lord, in mercy; sanctify thy fatherly correction to them; endue their souls with patience under their affliction, and with resignation to Thy blessed will comfort them with a sense of Thy goodness; lift up Thy countenance upon them, and give them peace; through Jesus Christ our Lord. Amen.

O GOD, whose days are without end, and whose mercies cannot be numbered; Make us, we beseech Thee, deeply sensible of the shortness and uncertainty of human life; and let Thy. Holy Spirit lead us through this vale of misery, in holiness and righteousness, all the days of our lives; That when we shall have served Thee in out generation, we may be gathered unto our fathers, having the testimony of a good conscience; in the communion of the catholic Church; in the confidence of a certain faith; in the comfort of a reasonable, religious, and holy hope; in favor with Thee our God, and in perfect charity with the world. All which we ask, through Jesus Christ our Lord. Amen.

GRANT, we beseech Thee, Almighty God,   that the words which we have heard this day with our outward ears, may, through Thy grace, be so grafted inwardly in our hearts, that they may bring forth in us the fruit of good living, to the honor and praise of Thy name, through Jesus Christ our Lord. Amen.

O GOD, Holy Ghost, Sanctifier of the Faithful, visit, we pray Thee, this Congregation with Thy love and favor; enlighten their minds more and more with the light of the everlasting Gospel; graft in their hearts a love of the truth; increase in them true religion; nourish them with all goodness and of Thy great mercy keep them in the same, O Blessed Spirit, whom, with the Father and the Son, together, we worship and glorify as one God, world without end. Amen.

In time of War and Tumults..

O ALMIGHTY God, the supreme Governor of all things, whose power no creature is able to resist, to whom it belongeth justly to punish sinners, and to be merciful to those who truly repent; Save and deliver us, we humbly beseech thee, from the hands of our enemies; that we, being armed with thy defense, may be preserved evermore from all perils, to glorify thee, who art the only giver of all victory; through the merits of thy Son, Jesus. Christ our Lord. Amen.

The Prayer to be said before a Fight against any Enemy.

O MOST powerful and glorious Lord God, the Lord of hosts, that rulest and commandest all things; Thou sittest in the throne judging right, and therefore we make our address to thy Divine Majesty in this our necessity, that thou wouldest take the cause into thine own hand, and judge between us and our enemies. Stir up thy strength, O Lord, and come and help us; for thou givest not alway the battle to the strong, but canst save by many or by few. O let not our sins cry against us for vengeance; (but hear us thy poor servants begging mercy, and imploring thy help, and that thou wouldest be a defense unto us against the face of the enemy. Make it appear that thou art our Saviour and mighty Deliverer, through Jesus Christ our Lord. Amen.

Thanksgiving for Victory.

O ALMIGHTY God, the Sovereign Commander of all the world, in whose hand is power and might, which none is able to withstand; We bless and magnify thy great and glorious Name for this happy Victory, the whole glory whereof we do ascribe to thee, who art the only giver of victory. And, we beseech thee, give us grace to improve this great mercy to thy glory, the advancement of thy Gospel, the honor of our country, and, as much as in us lieth, to the good of all mankind. And, we beseech thee, give us such a sense of this great mercy, as may engage us to a true thankfulness, such as may appear in our lives by an humble, holy; and obedient walking before thee all our day's; through Jesus Christ our Lord; to whom, with thee and the Holy Spirit, as for all thy mercies, so in particular for this Victory and Deliverance be all glory and honor, world without end. Amen.

A LMIGHTY God, the fountain of all wisdom, who knowest our necessities before we ask, and our ignorance in asking; We beseech thee to have compassion upon our infirmities; and those things, which for our unworthiness we dare not, and for our blindness we cannot ask, vouchsafe to give us, for the worthiness of thy Son Jesus Christ our Lord. Amen.

A Prayer for the Army and Navy.

O ETERNAL God; our Heavenly Father, who hast taught us to make prayers and supplications, and to give thanks for all men; We bless thee for those our fellow-citizens whom thou hast raised up to defend us against the assaults of our enemies by land and by sea. We commend them and all things belonging to them to thy Almighty protection. guard them, we beseech thee, from the dangers to which they are continually exposed by their lives and their health be precious in thy sight, and may thy mercy compass them on every side.

In the day of battle, do thou, the Lord of hosts, the giver of all victory, direct and shelter them, and endue them with such valor and skill, and crown them with such success, as may ensure to us all the advantages of an honorable peace.

May they ever cherish a grateful sense of thy mercies; and in thine own good time may they be restored to their homes, to enjoy the blessings which, under thy favor, their efforts shall have secured.

Grant this, we beseech thee, O merciful Father, through Jesus Christ our Mediator and Redeemer. Amen.

A Morning Prayer.

ALMIGHTY and everlasting GOD, in whom I live and move and have my being; I render thee my humble praises for thy preservation of me from the beginning of my life to the present day, and especially for having brought me in safety through the past night. And since it is of thy mercy, O gracious Father, that another day is added to my life, I here dedicate both my soul and body to thee and thy service; in a sober, righteous, and godly life: in which resolution, do thou; O merciful God, confirm and strengthen me, that, as I grow in age, I may grow in grace, and in the knowledge of our Lord and Saviour Jesus Christ.

But, O God, who knowest the weakness and corruption of our nature, and the manifold temptations which we daily meet with: I humbly beseech thee to have compassion on my infirmities, and to give me the constant assistance of thy Holy Spirit; that I may be effectually restrained from sin and excited to my duty. Imprint upon my heart such a dread of thy judgments, and such a grateful sense of thy goodness to me, as may make me both afraid and ashamed to offend thee. And above all, keep, in my mind a lively remembrance of that great day, in which I must give a strict account of my thoughts, words and actions; and according to the works done in the body, be eternally rewarded or punished, by him whom thou hast appointed the Judge of quick and dead, thy Son Jesus Christ our Lord.

In particular, I implore thy grace and protection during the ensuing day. Cleanse the thoughts of my heart by thy Holy Spirit, that I may perfectly love thee and direct me in all my doings with thy most gracious favor, and further me with thy continual help; that in all my works begun, continued and ended in thee, I may glorify thy holy name, and finally, by thy mercy; obtain everlasting life, through Jesus Christ our Lord.

Be pleased, O Lord, to take under thy fatherly care and protection my relations and friends. Make them all partakers of thy grace here, and of everlasting glory hereafter. Be favorable to our country. Let thy mercy embrace on every side, and let thy favor be its glory. Give wisdom from above to all in authority over us, and make us a people fearing thee and working righteousness. These things, and whatever else thou shalt see necessary and convenient for us, I humbly beg, through the merits and mediation of thy Son Jesus Christ our Lord and Saviour. Amen.

An Evening Prayer.

M OST merciful God, who art of purer eyes than to behold iniquity, and hast promised forgiveness to all those who. confess and forsake their sins, I come before thee in an humble sense of my own unworthiness, acknowledging my manifold transgressions. Make me deeply sensible of the great evil of them, and work in me an hearty contrition, that I may obtain forgiveness at thy hands for the sake of thy Son Jesus Christ, our only Saviour and Redeemer.

And lest I be drawn again into sin, vouchsafe me, I beseech thee, the direction and assistance of the Holy Spirit. Reform whatever is amiss in the temper and disposition of my soul, that no unclean thoughts, unlawful designs, or inordinate desires, may rest there; that I may be so preserved pure and blameless, unto the coming of our Lord and Saviour Jesus Christ.

And accept, O Lord, my intercessions for all mankind. Send down thy blessings, temporal and spiritual, upon all my relations, friends and neighbors. Be merciful to all who are in any trouble, and do thou, the God of pity; administer to them according to their several necessities, for his sake who went about doing good, thy Son, our Saviour, Jesus Christ.

To my prayers; O Lord, I join my unfeigned thanks for all thy mercies. Above all, I adore thee, for sending thy only Son into the world, to redeem me from sin and eternal death, and for giving me the knowledge and sense of my duty towards thee. I bless thee for thy patience with me, notwithstanding my many and great provocations, for all the directions, assistances and comforts, of thy Holy Spirit; and for thy continual care and watchful providence over me through the whole course of my life. I beseech thee to continue thy gracious protection to me this night. Defend me from all dangers and mischiefs, and fit me for the duties of the following day. Make me ever mindful of the time when I shall lie down in the dust, and grant me grace always to live in such a state that I may never be afraid to die, so that living and dying, I may be thine, through the merits and satisfaction of thy Son, Christ Jesus, in whose name I offer up these my imperfect prayers. Amen.

A Prayer for a Sick Person.

O FATHER of mercies and God of all comfort, our only help in time of need, I flee to thee for succor. Look down in pity and compassion on thy afflicted servant. May thy fatherly correction have its due influence upon me, by leading me to consider how frail and uncertain my life is, that I may apply my heart unto that heavenly wisdom which will bring me to everlasting life. Give me unfeigned repentance for all my sins. Make me know and feel that there is none other name given to man in whom, and through whom, I may receive health and salvation, but only the name of our Lord Jesus Christ, that through steadfast faith in him my sins may be done away by thy mercy, and my pardon sealed in heaven. Comfort me with a sense of thy goodness; preserve me from the temptations of the enemy; give me patience under my affliction; and in thy good time restore me to health, and enable me to lead the residue of my life in thy fear and glory. Or else give me grace so to take thy visitation, that, after this painful life is ended, I may dwell with thee in life everlasting, through Jesus Christ our Lord. Amen.

Thanksgiving for Recovery from Sickness.

O GOD, who art the giver of life, of health, and of safety, who bringest down to the grave and bringest up again, I bless thy wonderful goodness that thou hast been pleased to send me seasonable relief, and deliver me from my bodily affliction. Gracious art thou, O Lord, and full of compassion to the children of men. May my heart be duly impressed with a sense of thy merciful goodness, and may I devote the residue of my days to an humble, holy, and obedient walking before thee; through Jesus Christ our Lord. Amen.

———————

THE ORDER OF
CONFIRMATION,
OR LAYING ON OF HANDS UPON THOSE WHO ARE BAPTIZED, AND COME TO YEARS OF DISCRETION.

¶ *Upon the day appointed, all that are to be then confirmed; being placed and standing in order before the Bishop; he, or some other Minister appointed by him, shalt read this Preface following:*

TO the end that Confirmation may be ministered to the more edifying of such as shall receive it, the Church hath thought good to order, That none shall be confirmed, but such as can say the Creed, the Lord's Prayer and the Ten Commandments; and can also answer to such other Questions, as in the short Catechism are contained; which order is very convenient to be observed; to the end, that children, being now come to the years of discretion, and having learned what their Godfathers and Godmothers promised for them in Baptism, may themselves, with their own mouth and consent, openly before the Church, ratify and confirm the same; and also promise, that, by the grace of God, they will evermore endeavor themselves faithfully to observe such things, as they, by their own confession, have assented unto.

¶ *Then shall the Bishop say,*

DO ye here, in the presence of God, and of this congregation, renew the solemn promise and vow that ye made, or that was made in your name, at your Baptism; ratifying and confirming the same; and acknowledging yourselves bound to believe and to do all those things which ye then undertook, or your Sponsors then undertook for you?

¶ *And every one shall audibly answer,*

I do.

Bishop.

OUR help is in the Name of the Lord;

Answer. Who hath made heaven and earth.

Bishop. Blessed be the Name of the Lord;

Answer. Henceforth, world without end.

Bishop. Lord, hear our prayer.

Answer. And let our cry come unto thee.

Bishop. Let us pray.

ALMIGHTY and everlasting God, who hast vouchsafed to regenerate these thy servants by Water and the Holy Ghost, and hast given unto them forgiveness of all their sins; Strengthen them, we beseech thee, O Lord, with the Holy Ghost, the Comforter, and daily increase in them thy manifold gifts of grace; the spirit of wisdom and understanding, the spirit of counsel and ghostly strength, the spirit of knowledge and true godliness; and fill them, O Lord, with the spirit of thy holy fear, now and for ever. *Amen.*

¶ *Then all of them in order kneeling before the Bishop, he shall lay his hands upon the head of every one severally, saying,*

DEFEND, O Lord, this thy Child [or, *this thy Servant*] with thy heavenly grace; that *he* may continue thine for ever; and daily increase in thy Holy Spirit more and more, until *he* come unto thy everlasting kingdom. Amen.

Then shall the Bishop say,

The Lord be with you.

Answer. And with thy spirit.

And all kneeling down, the Bishop shall add,

Let us pray.

OUR Father, who art in heaven, Hallowed   be thy Name. Thy kingdom come. Thy   will be done on earth, As it is in heaven. Give us this day our daily bread. And forgive us our trespasses, As we forgive those who trespass against us. And lead us not into temptation; But deliver us from evil. Amen.

And these Collects:

ALMIGHTY and ever living God, who makest us both to will and to do those things which are good, and acceptable unto thy Divine Majesty; We make our humble supplications unto thee for these thy servants, upon whom, after the example of thy holy Apostles, we have now laid our hands, to certify them, by this sign, of thy favor and gracious goodness towards them. Let thy fatherly hand, we beseech thee, ever be over them; let thy Holy Spirit ever be with them; and so lead them in the knowledge and obedience of thy Word, that in the end they may obtain everlasting life; through our Lord Jesus Christ, who with thee and the Holy Ghost liveth and reigneth, ever one God, world without end. *Amen.*

O ALMIGHTY Lord, and everlasting God, vouchsafe, we beseech thee, to direct, sanctify, and govern, both our hearts and bodies, in the ways of thy laws, and in the works of thy commandments; that, through thy most mighty protection both here and ever, we may be preserved in body and soul; through our Lord and Saviour Jesus Christ. *Amen.*

¶ *Then the Bishop shall bless them, saying thus,*

THE Blessing of God Almighty, the Father, the Son, and the Holy Ghost, be upon you, and remain with you for ever. Amen.

¶ *And there shall none be admitted to the Holy Communion, until such time as he be confirmed, or be ready and desirous to be confirmed.*

PSALMS

----

1   **C. M.**   **(1 of P. B.)**

HOW blest is he, Who ne'er consents
 By ill advice to walk,
  Nor stands in sinners' ways, nor sits
   Where men profanely talk;

2 But makes the perfect law of GOD
 His business and delight;
Devoutly reads therein by day,
 And meditates by night.

3 Like some fair tree, which, fed by streams,
 With timely fruit does bend,
He still shall flourish, and success
 All his designs attend.

4 Ungodly men, and their attempts,
 No lasting root shall find;
Untimely blasted, and dispersed
 Like chaff before the wind.

5 Their guilt shall strike the wicked dumb
 Before their Judge's face:
No formal hypocrite shall then
 Among the saints have place.

6 For GOD approves the just man's ways;
 To happiness they tend;

But sinners, and the paths they tread,

    Shall both in ruin end.

2   C. M.   (18 of P. B.)

THE LORD himself, the mighty LORD,

    Vouchsafes to be my guide;

The shepherd, by whose constant care

    My wants are all supplied.

2 In tender grass he makes me feed,

    And gently there repose;

Then leads me to cool shades, and where

    Refreshing water flows.

3 He does my wand'ring soul reclaim,

    And, to his endless praise,

Instruct with humble zeal to walk

    In his most righteous ways.

4 I pass the gloomy vale of death,

    From fear and danger free;

For there his aiding rod and staff

    Defend and comfort me.

5 Since God doth thus his wondrous love

    Through all my life extend,

That life to him I will devote,

    And in his temple spend.

3   **L. M.**   **(79 of P. B.)**

WITH one consent let all the earth

To God their cheerful voices raise;

Glad homage pay with awful mirth,

And sing before him songs of praise:

2 Convinced that he is GOD alone,

From whom both we and all proceed;

We whom he chooses for his own,

The flock that he vouchsafes to feed.

3 O enter then his temple gate,

Thence to his courts devoutly press;

And still your grateful hymns repeat,

And still his Name with praises bless.

4 For he's the LORD, supremely good,

His mercy is forever sure;

His truth, which always firmly stood,

To endless ages shall endure.

4   **S. M.**   **(82 of P. B.)**

O BLESS the LORD, my soul,

His grace to thee proclaim;

And all that is within me, join

To bless his holy Name.

2 O bless the LORD, my soul,

His mercies bear in mind;

Forget not all his benefits,

   Who is to thee so kind.

3 He pardons all thy sins,

   Prolongs thy feeble breath;

He healeth thine infirmities,

   And ransoms thee from death.

4 He feeds thee with his love,

   Upholds thee with his truth;

And, like the eagle's, he renews

   The vigor of thy youth.

6 Then bless the LORD, my soul,

   His grace, his love proclaim;

Let all that is within me join

   To bless his holy Name.

HYMNS

G REAT GOD! with wonder and with praise
On all thy works I look;
But still thy wisdom, power, and grace,
Shine brightest in thy book.

2 The stars, that in their courses roll,
Have much instruction given;
But thy good word informs my soul
How I may soar to heaven.

3 The fields provide me food, and show
The goodness of the LORD;
But fruits of life and glory grow
In thy most holy word.

4 Here are my choicest treasures hid;
Here my best comfort lies;
Here my desires are satisfied, And here my hopes arise.

5 LORD, make me understand thy law,
Show what my faults have been;
And from thy Gospel let me draw
Pardon for all my sin.

6 Here would I learn how CHRIST has died
To save my soul from hell;
Not all the books on earth beside,

Such heavenly wonders tell.

7 Then let me love my Bible more,

And take a fresh delight,

By day to read these wonders o'er,

And meditate by night.

6   S.M.   (13 of P. B.)

Job 9:2-6.

A H, how shall fallen man
Be just before his God!

If he contend in righteousness

We sink beneath his rod.

2 If be our ways should mark,

With strict inquiring eyes,

Could we for one of thousand faults,

A just excuse devise?

3 All-seeing, powerful GOD!

Who can with thee contend?

Or who that tries the unequal strife,

Shall prosper in the end?

4 The mountains, in thy wrath,

Their ancient seats forsake:

The trembling earth deserts her place,

Her rooted pillars shake:

5 Ah, how shall guilty man

Contend with such a GOD?

None, none can meet him, and escape,

But through the Saviour's blood.

7   C. M.   (16 of P. B.)

SALVATION! O the joyful sound,

Glad tidings to our ears;

A sovereign balm for every wound,

A cordial for our fears.

2 Salvation! buried once in sin,

At hell's dark door we lay;

But now we rise by grace divine,

And see a heav'nly day.

3 Salvation! let the echo fly

The spacious earth around;

While all the armies of the sky

Conspire to raise the sound.

4 Salvation! O thou bleeding Lamb,

To thee the praise belongs:

Our hearts shall kindle at thy name,

Thy name inspire our songs.

Chorus for the end of each verse.

Glory, honor, praise and power

Be unto the Lamb forever!

JESUS CHRIST is our Redeemer!

Hallelujah, praise the LORD!

8   S. M.   (32 of P. B.)

WELCOME, sweet day of rest,
  That saw the LORD arise;
Welcome to this reviving breast,
  And these rejoicing eyes.
2 The king himself comes near
  To feast his saints to-day;
Here may we sit, and see him here,
  And love, and praise, and pray.
3 One day amidst the place
  Where JESUS is within,
Is better than ten thousand days
  Of pleasure and of sin.
4 My willing soul would stay
  In such a frame as this,
Till it is called to soar away
  To everlasting bliss.

9   C. M.   (43 of P. B.)
                Luke 3:8-15.

WHILE shepherds watched their flocks by night,
  All seated on the ground,
The angel of the LORD came down,

And glory shone around.

2 "Fear not," said he, for mighty dread

Had seized their troubled mind;

"Glad tidings of great joy I bring

To you, and all mankind.

3 To you, in David's town, this day

Is born, of David's line,

The Saviour, who is CHRIST the Lord,

And this shall be the sign:

4 "The heav'nly babe you there shall find,

To human view display'd,

All meanly wrapt in swathing bands,

And in a manger laid."

5 Thus spake the seraph, and forthwith

Appear'd a shining throng

Of angels, praising GOD, who thus

Address'd their joyful song:

6 "All glory be to GOD on high,

And to the earth be peace;

Good will, henceforth, from heaven to men,

Begin and never cease."

10   L.M.   (57 of P. B.)

MY. GOD, permit me not to be

A stranger to myself and thee:

Amidst a thousand thoughts 1 rove,

Forgetful of my highest love.

2 Why should my passions mix with earth,

And thus debase my heav'nly birth?

Why should I cleave to things below,

And all my purest joys forego?

3 Call me away from flesh and sense

Thy grace, O LORD, can draw me thence:

I would obey the voice divine,

And all inferior joys resign.

11   C. M.   (58 of P. B.)

ALAS, what hourly dangers rise!

What snares beset my way!

To heaven, O let me lift mine eyes,

And hourly watch and pray.

2 How oft my mournful thoughts complain,

And melt in flowing tears!

My weak resistance, ah, how vain!

How strong my foes and fears!

3 O gracious GOD, in whom I live,

My feeble efforts aid;

Help me to watch, and pray and strive,

Though trembling and afraid.

Increase my faith, increase my hope,

When foes and fears prevail;

And bear my fainting spirit up,

  Or soon my strength will fail.

5 Whene'er temptations fright my heart,

 Or lure my feet aside,

My GOD, thy powerful aid impart,

  My guardian and my guide.

6 O keep me in thy heav'nly way,

  And bid the tempter flee;

And let me never, never stray

  From happiness and thee.

12   C. M.   (59 of P. B.)

HOW oft, alas! this wretched heart.

Has wander'd from the Lord!

How oft my roving thoughts depart,

  Forgetful of his word !

2 Yet sovereign mercy calls, "Return;"

  Dear LORD, and may I come?

My vile ingratitude, I mourn;

  O take the wand'rer home.

3 And canst thou, wilt thou yet forgive,

  And bid my crimes remove?

And shall a pardon'd rebel live

  To speak thy wondrous love?

4 Almighty grace, thy healing power,

How glorious, how divine!

That can to life and bliss restore

So vile a heart as mine.

5 Thy pard'ning love, so free, so sweet,

Dear Saviour, I adore:

6 keep me at thy sacred feet,

And let me rove no more.

13   **L. M.**   (62 of P. B.)

WHEN I survey the wondrous cross,

On which the prince of glory died,

My richest gain I count but loss,

And pour contempt on all my pride.

2 Forbid it, Lord, that I should boast,

Save in the cross of Christ my GOD:

All the vain things that charm me most,

I sacrifice them to thy blood.

3 See, from his head, his hands, his feet,

Sorrow and love flow mingled down:

Did e'er such love and sorrow meet?

Or thorns compose a Saviour's crown?

4 Were the whole realm of nature mine,

That were a tribute far too small;

Love so amazing, so divine,

Demands my life, my soul, my all.

14   III. 1.   (69 of P. B.)

CHRIST the Lord is risen today,
    Sons of men and angels say:
Raise your joys and triumphs high,
        Sing, ye heavens, and earth reply!

2 Love's redeeming work is done,
    Fought the fight, the vict'ry won:
Jesus' agony is o'er,
    Darkness veils the earth no more.

3 Vain the stone, the watch, the seal,
    CHRIST has burst the gates of hell;
Death in vain forbids him rise,
    CHRIST hath open'd paradise.

4 Soar we now where CHRIST hath led,
    Following our exalted Head;
Made like him, like him we rise;
    Ours the cross, the grave, the skies.

15   C. M.   (75 of P. B.)

COME, Holy Spirit, Heav'nly Dove,
    With all thy quick'ning powers,
Kindle a flame of sacred love
    In these cold hearts of ours.

2 See bow we grovel here below,
    Fond of these earthly toys:

Our souls, how heavily they go,

  To reach eternal joys.

3 In vain we tune our lifeless songs,

  In vain we strive to rise:

Hosannas languish on our tongues,

  And our devotion dies.

4 Come, Holy Spirit, Heav'nly Dove,

  With all thy quick'ning powers;

Come, shed abroad a Saviour's love,

  And that shall kindle ours.

16   S. M.   (88 of P. B.)

Ephesians 6:10-13

SOLDIERS of CHRIST, arise,

And put your armor on,

Strong in the strength which GOD supplies,

  Through his eternal Son.

2 Strong in the LORD of hosts,

  And in his mighty power,

Who in the strength of Jesus trusts,

  Is more than conqueror.

3 Stand then in his great might,

  With all his strength endued;

And take to arm you for the fight,

  The panoply of GOD.

4 That, having all things done,

And all your conflicts past,

Ye may behold your vict'ry won,

   And stand complete at last.

17   L. M.   (89 of P. B.)

O HAPPY day! that stays my choice

   On thee my Saviour and my God!

Well may this glowing heart rejoice,

   And tell thy goodness all abroad.

2 O happy bond! that seals my vows,

   To him who merits all my love;

Let cheerful anthems fill his house,

   While to his sacred throne I move.

3 Tis done, the great transaction's done;

   Deign, gracious Lord, to make me thine;

Help me, through grace, to follow on,

   Glad to confess thy voice divine.

4 Here rest, my oft-divided heart,

   Fix'd on thy GOD, thy Saviour, rest;

Who with the world would grieve to part,

   When call'd on angel's food to feast?

5 High heaven, that heard the solemn vow,

   That vow renew'd shall daily hear,

Till in life's latest hour I bow,

   And bless in death a bond so dear.

18   C. M.   (65 of P. B.)

AND are we now brought near to GOD,
    Who once at distance stood?
And, to effect this glorious change,
    Did JESUS shed his blood?

2 O for a song of ardent praise,
    To bear our souls above!
What should allay our lively hope,
    Or damp our flaming love?

8 Then let us join the heav'nly choirs,
    To praise our heav'nly King:
O may that love which spread this board,
    Inspire us while we sing:

4 "Glory to GOD in highest strains,
    And to the earth be peace;
Good will from heaven to men is come,
    And let it never cease."

19   III. 1.   (128 of P. B.)

SINNERS, torn, why will ye die?
    GOD, your Maker, asks you why:
    GOD, who did your being give,
    Made you with himself to live:
He the fatal cause demands,

Asks the works of his own hands:

Why, ye thankless creatures, why

    Will ye cross his love; and die?

2 Sinners, turn, why will ye die?

    God, your Saviour, asks you why:

He, who did your souls retrieve,

    Died himself that ye might live.

Will you let him die in vain?

    Crucify your Lord again?

Why, ye ransom'd sinners, why

    Will ye slight his grace, and die?

3 Sinners, turn, why will ye die?

    God, the Spirit, asks you why:

He who all your lives hath strove,

    Woo'd you to embrace his love.

Will ye not his grace receive?

    Will ye still refuse to live?

0, ye dying sinners, why,

    Why will ye for over die?

20   III. 1.   (129 of P. B.)

HASTEN, sinner, to be wise;

Stay not for the morrow's sun;

Wisdom, if you still despise,

    Harder is it to be won.

2 Hasten, mercy to implore;

   Stay not for the morrow's sun;

Lest thy season should be o'er,

   Ere this evening's stage be run.

3 Hasten, sinner, to return;

   Stay not for the morrow's sun;

Lest thy lamp should cease to burn,

   Ere salvation's work is done.

4 Hasten, sinner, to be blest;

   Stay not for the morrow's sun;

Lest perdition thee arrest,

   Ere the morrow is begun.

21   **S. M.**   **(131 of P. B.)**

Rev. 22:17-20.

THE Spirit, in our hearts,

   Is whispering sinner, come!

The Bride, the Church of CHRIST proclaims

   To all his children, come

2 Let him that heareth say

   To all about him, come!

Let him that thirsts for righteousness,

   To CHRIST, the fountain, come!

3 Yes, whosoever will,

   O let him freely come,

And freely drink the stream of life:

Tis JESUS bids him come.

4 Lo, JESUS, who invites,

Declares, I quickly come,

LORD, even so; I wait thy hour;

JESUS, my Saviour, come!

22   C. M.   (133 of P. B.)

APPROACH, my soul, the mercy-seat,

Where JESUS answers prayer;

There humbly fall before his feet,

For none can perish there.

2 Thy promise is my only plea,

With this I venture nigh:

Thou callest burdened souls to thee,

And such, O LORD, am I.

3 Bow'd down beneath a load of sin,

By Satan sorely press'd,

By war without, and fear within,

I come to thee for rest.

4 Be thou my shield and hiding-place;

That, shelter'd near thy side,

I may my fierce accuser face,

And tell him, "Thou hast died."

5 Oh! wondrous love! to bleed and die,

To hear the cross and shame,

That guilty sinners, such as I,

   Might plead thy gracious name.

   23   **C. M.**   **(134 of P. B.)**

PRAYER is the soul's sincere desire,
   Utter'd or unexpress'd:
The motion of a hidden fire,
   That trembles in the breast.

2 Prayer is the burden of a sigh,
   The falling of a tear,
The upward glancing of an eye,
   When none but GOD is near.

8 Prayer is the simplest form of speech
   That infant lips can try;
Prayer, the sublimest strains that reach
   The majesty on high.

4 Prayer is the Christian's vital breath,
   The Christian's native air,
The watch-word at the gate of death;
   He enters heaven with prayer.

5 Prayer is the contrite sinner's voice,
   Returning from his ways;
While angels in their songs rejoice,
   And cry, "Behold, he prays!"

6 In prayer, on earth, the saints are one,

    They're one in word and mind,

When with the Father and the Son

    Sweet fellowship they find.

7 O thou, by whom we come to GOD,

    The life, the truth, the way,

The path of prayer thyself hast trod:

    LORD, teach us how to pray.

24   L. M.   (137 of P. B.)

O THAT my load of sin were gone,

    O that I could at last submit,

At JESUS' feet to lay it down,

    To lay my soul at JESUS' feet!

2 Rest for my soul I long to find;

    Saviour of all, if mine thou art,

Give me thy meek and lowly mind,

    And stamp thine image on my heart.

3 Break off the yoke of inbred sin,

    And fully set my spirit free;

I cannot rest till pure within,

    Till I am wholly lost in thee.

4 Fain would I learn of thee, my GOD;

    Thy light and easy burden prove,

The cross all stain'd with hallow'd blood,

The labor of thy dying love.

5 I would, but thou must give the power,

My heart front every sin release:

Bring near, bring near the joyful hour,

And fill me with thy perfect peace,

25　　　　　**III. 1.**　　　　**(143 of P. B.)**

Christ our Refuge.

JESUS, Saviour of my soul,

Let me to thy bosom fly,

While the waves of trouble roll,

While the tempest still is high;

Hide me, O my Saviour, hide,

Till the storm of life is past;

Safe into the haven guide;

O receive my soul at last.

2 Other refuge have I none,

Hangs my helpless soul on thee;

Leave, ah! leave me not alone,

Still support and comfort me:

All my trust on thee is stay'd,

All my hope from thee I bring;

Cover my defenseless head

With the shadow of thy wing.

26   IV. 4.   (144 of P. B.)

H OW firm a foundation, ye saints of the LORD,

    Is laid for your faith in his excellent word!

What more can he say than to you he hath said,

    You who unto JESUS for refuge have fled:

2 Fear not, I am with thee, O be not die-
may'd,

    I, I am thy GOD, and will still give thee aid;

I'll strengthen thee, help thee, and cause thee to stand,

    Upheld by my righteous, omnipotent hand.

3 When through the deep waters I call thee to go,

    The rivers of woe shall not thee overflow;

For I will be with thee thy troubles to bless,

    And sanctify to thee thy deepest distress.

4 When through fiery trials thy pathway shall lie,

    My grace, all-sufficient, shall be thy supply;

The flame shall not hurt thee, I only design

    Thy dross to consume, and thy gold to refine.

5 The soul that to JESUS hath fled for repose,

    I will not, I will not desert to his foes:

That soul, though all hell shall endeavor to shake,

    I'll never—no, never—no, never forsake,

27   III. 1.   (146 of P. B.)

C HILDREN of the heav'nly King,

As we journey let us sing;

Sing the Saviour's worthy praise,

Glorious in his works and ways.

2 We are trav'ling home to GOD

In the way the fathers trod;

They are happy now, and we

Soon their happiness shall see.

3 Banish'd once, by sin betrayed,

CHRIST our advocate was made;

Pardon'd now, no more we roam,

CHRIST conducts us to our home.

4 LORD, obediently we'll go,

Gladly leaving all below;

Only thou our leader be,

And we still will follow thee.

28   C. M.   (147 of P. B.)

WHEN I can read my title clear.

To mansions in the skies,

I'll bid farewell to every fear,

And wipe my weeping eyes.

2 Should earth against my soul engage,

And fiery darts be hurl'd,

Then I can smile at Satan's rage,

And face a frowning world.

3 Let cares like a wild deluge come,

Let storms of sorrow fall;

So I but safely reach my home,

My GOD, my heaven, my all:

4 There, anchor'd safe, my weary soul

Shall find eternal rest;

Nor storms shall beat, nor billows roll

Across my peaceful breast.

29   C. M.   (174 of P. B.)

Renouncing the World.

L ET worldly minds the world pursue,

It has no charms for me;

Once I admired its follies too,

But grace has set me free.

2 Those follies now no longer please,

No more delight afford;

Far from my heart be joys like these,

Now I have known the LORD.

3 As by the light of op'ning day

The stars are all conceal'd,

So earthly pleasures fade away

When JESUS is reveal'd.

4 Creatures no more divide my choice,

I bid them all depart;

His name, and love, and gracious voice

   Shall fix my roving heart.

5 Now, Loan, I would be thine alone,

   And wholly live to thee;

Yet worthless still myself I own,

   Thy worth is all my plea.

30   L. M.   (175 of P B.)

Not ashamed of Christ.

J*ESUS!* and shall it ever be,

   A mortal man ashamed of thee:

Ashamed of thee, whom angels praise,

   Whose glories shine through endless days?

2 Ashamed of JESUS! sooner far

   Let night disown each radiant star;

Tis midnight with my soul, till he,

   Bright Morning Star, bid darkness flee.

3 Ashamed of JESUS! O, as soon Let morning blush to own the sun; He sheds the beams of light divine O'er this benighted soul of mine.

4 Ashamed of JESUS! that dear friend

   On whom my hopes of heaven depend:

No; when I blush, be this my shame,

   That I no more revere his name.

5 Ashamed of JESUS! empty pride;

   I'll boast a Saviour crucified;

And, O, may this my portion be,

My Saviour not ashamed of me.

31   **III. 3.**   **(177 of P. B.)**

Prayer for Guidance.

GUIDE me, O thou great JEHOVAH,

Pilgrim through this barren land;

I am weak, but thou art mighty;

Hold me with thy powerful hand.

2 Open now the crystal fountains

Whence the living waters flow;

Let the fiery, cloudy pillar,

Lead me all my journey through.

3 Feed me with the heav'nly manna

In this barren wilderness;

Be my sword, and shield, and banner;

Be the LORD my righteousness.

4 When I tread the verge of Jordan,

Bid my anxious fears subside;

Death of death, and hell's destruction,

Land me safe on Canaan's side.

32   **S. M.**   **(179 of P. B.)**

Duties.

A CHARGE to keep I have,

A GOD to glorify;

A never dying soul to save,

   And fit it for the sky:

2 From youth to hoary age,

   My calling to fulfill:

O may it all my powers engage

   To do my Master's will.

3 Arm me with jealous care,

   As in thy sight to live,

And, oh thy servant, LORD, prepare,

   A strict account to give:

4 Help me to watch and pray,

   And on thyself rely;

Assured if I my trust betray,

   I shall for ever die.

33   **C. M.**   **(180 of P. B.)**

"Forgetting those things which are behind, &c.
Phil. 3:13-14.

AWAKE, my soul, stretch every nerve,

   And press with vigor on;

A heav'nly race demands thy zeal,

   And an immortal crown.

2 A cloud of witnesses around

   Hold thee in full survey;

Forget the steps already trod,

   And onward urge thy way.

3 'Tis GOD'S all animating voice

  That calls thee from on high,

Tis his own hand presents the prize

  To thine uplifted eye.

4 Then wake, my soul, stretch every nerve,

  And press with vigor on;

A heav'nly race demands thy zeal,

  And an immortal crown.

34   C. M.   (189 of P. B.)

HARK! from the tombs a mournful sound,
Mine ears attend the cry;

  "Ye living men, come view the ground

  Where you must shortly lie.

2 Princes, this clay must be your bed,

  In spite of all your towers;

The tall, the wise, the rev'rend head

  Must lie as low as ours."

3 Great GOD! is this our certain doom?

  And are we still secure?

Still walking downward to the tomb,

  And yet prepare no more?

4 Grant us the power of quick'ning grace

  To raise our souls to thee,

That we may view thy glorious face

To all eternity.

35   L. M. (168 of P. B.)

Evening Hymn.

GLORY to thee, my GOD, this night,
  For all the blessings of the light:
Keep me, O keep me, King of kings,
  Under thine own almighty wings.

2 Forgive me, LORD, for thy dear Son,
  The ills that I this day have done:
That with the world, myself, and thee,
  I, ere I sleep, at peace may be.

3 Teach me to live, that I may dread
  The grave as little as my bed;
Teach me to die, that so I may
  Triumphing rise at the last day.

4 O may my soul on thee repose,
  And with sweet sleep mimic eyelids close;
Sleep, that may me more vig'rous make
  To serve my GOD, when I awake.

6 When in the night I sleepless lie,
  My soul with heav'nly thoughts supply:
Let no ill dreams disturb my rest,
  No powers of darkness me molest,

6 O when shall I, in endless day,

For ever chase dark sleep away,

And hymns divine with angels sing,

   Glory to thee, eternal King.

7 Praise GOD, from whom all blessings flow,

Praise him, all creatures here below;

Praise him above, angelic host;

Praise Father, Son, and Holy Ghost.

36   L. M.   (163 of P. B.)

"I have set God always before me."—Psalm 16:9

SAVIOUR, when night involves the skies,

   My soul, adoring, turns to thee;

Thee, self abased in mortal guise,

   And wrapt in shades of death for me.

2 On thee my waking raptures dwell,

   When crimson gleams the east adorn;

Thee, victor of the grave and hell;

   Thee, source of life's eternal morn.

3 When noon her throne in light arrays,

   To thee my soul triumphant springs;

Thee, throned in glory's endless blaze,

   Thee, LORD of lords, and King of kings.

4 O'er earth, when shades of evening steal,

   To death and thee my thoughts I give;

To death, whose power I soon must feel,

To thee, with whom I trust to live.

ADDITIONAL
37   C. M.

"I will sing praise unto thy name forever." — Ps. 61:8.

JESUS, I love thy charming name;
  Tis music to my ear;
Fain would I sound it out so loud
  That earth and heaven might hear;

2 Yes,—thou art precious to my soul,
  My transport and my trust;
Jewels to thee are gaudy toys,
  And gold is sordid dust.

3 Thy grace shall dwell upon my heart,
  And shed its fragrance there;
The noblest balm of all its wounds,
  The cordial of its care.

4 I'll speak the honors of thy name
  With my last lab'ring breath;
Then, speechless, clasp thee In my arms,
  The antidote of death.

38   C. M.

"Being justified by his blood, we shall be saved from wrath through him."— **Romans v. 9.**

T HERE is a fountain, filled with blood,

Drawn from Immanuel's veins,

And sinners plunged beneath that flood

Lose all their guilty stains.

2 The dying thief rejoiced to see

That fountain in his day;

And there may I, tho' vile as he,

Wash all my sins away.

3 Dear dying Lamb, thy precious blood

Shall never lose its power,

Till all the ransomed church of God

Be saved, to sin no more.

4 E'er since, by faith, I saw the stream

Thy flowing wounds supply,

Redeeming love has been my theme,

And shall be till I die.

7 Then, in a nobler, sweeter song,

I'll sing thy power to save;

When this poor lisping, stammering tongue

Lies silent in the grave.

39   L. M.

"And him that cometh unto me, I will in no wise cast out."—**John 6:37.**

JUST as I am, without one plea,

But that thy blood was shed for me,

And that thou bid'st me came to thee,

O Lamb of God, I come! I come!

2 Just as I am, and waiting not

To rid my soul of one dark blot,

To thee, whose blood can cleanse each spot,

O Lamb of God, I come! I come!

3 Just as I am, though tossed about

With many a conflict, many a doubt,

With fears within and wars without,

O Lamb of God, I come! I come!

4 Just as I am, poor, wretched, blind,

Sight, riches, healing of the mind,

Yea, all I need, in thee to find,

O Lamb of God, I come! I come!

5 Just as I am—thou wilt receive,

Wilt welcome, pardon, cleanse, relieve,

Because thy promise I believe,

O Lamb of God, I come! I come!

6 Just as I am—thy love unknown

But broken every barrier down;

Now to he thine, yea, thine alone,

O Lamb of God, I come! I come!

40   C. M.

"Christ died for our sins."—1 Cor. 15:3.

ALAS! and did my Saviour bleed!

And did my sovereign die!

Would he devote that sacred head

For such a worm as I?

2 Was it for crimes that I have done,

He groaned upon the tree

Amazing pity! grace unknown!

And love beyond degree!

3 Well might the sun in darkness hide

And shut his glories in;

When Christ, the mighty Maker, died

For man the creature's sin.

4 Thus might I hide my blushing face

While his dear cross appears:

Dissolve my heart in thankfulness,

And melt my eyes to tears.

5 But drops of grief can ne'er repay

The debt of love I owe;

Here, Lord, I give myself away,

Tis all that I can do.

41   L. M.

"In whom we have boldness and access with confidence by the faith of him."—Eph. 3:12.

JESUS, my all, to heaven is gone;

　　He whom I fix my hopes upon;

His track I see, and I'll pursue

　　The narrow way, till him I view.

2 This is the way I long have sought,

　　And mourned because I found it not;

My grief a burden long has been,

　　Because I was not saved from sin.

3 The more I strove against its power,

I felt its weight and guilt the more;

Till late I heard my Saviour say,

"Come hither, soul, I am the way."

4 Lo ! glad I come; and thou blest Lamb

　　Shall take me to thee as I am;

Nothing but sin have I to give,

　　Nothing but love shall I receive.

5 Then will I tell to sinners round,

　　What a dear Saviour I have found;

I'll point to thy redeeming blood,

　　And say, "Behold the way to God."

42   C. M.

"He shall call upon me; and I will answer him."

Psalm 91:15.

C OME, humble sinner, in whose breast
  A thousand thoughts revolve;
  Come, with your guilt and fear oppressed,
    And make this last resolve;

2 I'll go to Jesus, though my sin
    Hath like a mountain rose;
  I know his courts, I'll enter in,
    Whatever may oppose.

3 Perhaps he will admit my plea,
    Perhaps will hear my prayer;
  But if I perish, I will pray,
    And perish only there.

4 I can but perish if I go;
    I am resolved to try;
  For if I stay away, I know
    I must forever die.

43   7s.

"Lovest thou me — John 21:16.

H ARK, my soul ! it is the Lord,
    Tis thy Saviour, hear his word;

Jesus speaks, and speaks to thee;

   "Say, poor sinner, lov'st thou me?"

2 "I delivered thee when bound,

   And when wounded, healed thy wound;

Sought thee wandering, set thee right,

   Turned thy darkness into light.

3 "Mine is an unchanging love,

   Higher than the heights above;

Deeper than the depths beneath,

   Free and faithful, strong as death.

4 "Thou shalt see my glory soon,

   When the work of grace is done;

Partner of my throne shall he;

   Say, poor sinner, lov'st thou me?"

5 Lord, it is my chief complaint,

   That my love is weak and faint;

Yet I love thee and adore;

   O for grace to love thee more..

44   C. M.

F OR mercies countless as the sands,

   Which daily I receive

From Jesus, my Redeemer's hands,

   My soul, what canst thou give?

2 Alas! from such a heart as mine,

   What can I bring him forth?

My best is stained and dyed with sin,

My all is nothing worth.

3 Yet this acknowledgment I'll make

For all be has bestowed:

Salvation's sacred cup I'll tare

And call upon my God.

4 The best return for one like Me,

So wretched and so poor,

Is from his gifts to draw a plea

And ask him still for more.

45   8, 7, 4.

"Come unto me, all ye that labor and are heavy laden, and t will give you rest."—Matt. 11:28.

COME, ye sinners, poor and needy;

Weak and wounded, sick and sore;

Jesus ready stands to save you,

Full of mercy, love and power.

He is able,

He is willing; doubt no more.

2 Now, ye needy, come and welcome,

God's free bounty glorify;

True belief, and true repentance,

Every grace that brings you nigh.

Without money,

Come to Jesus Christ, and buy.

8 Let not conscience make you linger,

　Nor of fitness fondly dream!

All the fitness he requireth

　Is to feel your need of him.

This he gives you,

　Tis the Spirit's rising beam.

4 Come, ye weary, heavy laden,

　Lost and ruined by the fall,

If you terry till you're better,

　You will never come at all.

Not the righteous —

　Sinners, Jesus came to call.

5 Lo! the incarnate God, ascended,

　Pleads the merit of his blood,

Venture on him, venture wholly,

　Let no other trust intrude;

None but Jesus

　Can do helpless sinners good.

46

I NEED thee, precious Jesus, for I am full of sin;

　My soul is dark and guilty, my heart is dead within;

I need the cleansing fountain, where I can always flee —

　The blood of Christ most precious, the sinner's perfect plea.

2 I need thee, precious Jesus, for I am very poor;

A stranger and a pilgrim, I have no earthly store;

I need the love of Jesus to cheer me on the way,

To guide my doubting footsteps, to be my strength and stay.

3 I need thee, precious Jesus, I need a Friend like thee —

A Friend to soothe and sympathize, a Friend to care for me;

I need the heart of Jesus to feel each anxious care,

To tell me every want, and all my sorrows share.

4 I need thee, precious Jesus, for I am very blind —

A weak and foolish wanderer, with a dark and evil mind.

I need the light of Jesus to tread the thorny road,

To guide me safe to glory, where I shall see my God.

5 I need thee, precious Jesus, I need thee day by day,

To fill me with thy fullness, to lead me on my way;

I need thy Holy Spirit to teach me what I am,

To show me more of Jesus, to point me to the Lamb.

6 I need thee, precious Jesus, and hope to see thee soon,

Encircled with a rainbow, and seated on thy throne;

There, with thy blood-bought children, my joy shall ever be

To sing thy praises, Jesus, to gaze, my Lord, on thee.

47   8, 7, 4.

L ORD dismiss us with thy blessing,

Fill our hearts with joy and peace;

Let us each thy love possessing,

Triumph in redeeming grace;

O refresh us,

Traveling through this wilderness.

2 Thanks we give, and adoration

For the gospel's joyful sound;

May the fruits of shy salvation

In our hearts an I lives abound;

May thy presence

With us evermore be found.

DOXOLOGIES

L. M.

P RAISE God, from whom all blessings flow,
Praise him, all creatures here below;

Praise him above, angelic host;

Praise Father, Son, and Holy Ghost.

C. M.

T O Father, Son, and Holy Ghost,
The God whom we adore,

Be glory, as it was of old,

And shall be evermore

L. M.

TO Father, Son, and Holy Ghost,

   The God whom earth and heaven adore,

   Be glory, as it was of old,

   Is now, and shall be evermore.

S. M.

TO God, the Father, Son;
         And Spirit, glory be,
   As 'twas, and is, and shall be so

   To all eternity.

7s.

HOLY Father, holy Son,

   Holy Spirit three in One!

   Glory, as of old, to thee

   Now and evermore shall be.

APPENDIX

A full Evening Prayer is formed by omitting the "Venite," "Te Deum" and "Jubilate," and using the following Psalms and Collects in their proper places.

After the first lesson:

Psalm 98.

O SING unto the Lord a new song; for he hath done marvelous things.

2 With his own right hand and with his holy arm, hath he gotten himself the victory.

3 The Lord declared his salvation; his righteousness hath he openly showed in the sight of the heathen.

4 Ile hath remembered his mercy and truth toward the house of Israel; and all the ends of the world have seen the salvation of our God.

5 Show yourselves joyful unto the Lord, all ye lands; sing, rejoice, and give thanks.

6. Praise the Lord upon the harp; sing to the harp with a psalm of thanksgiving.

7 With trumpets also and shawns, O show yourselves joyful unto the Lord, the King.

8 Let the sea make a noise, and all that therein is; the round World, and they that dwell therein.

9 Let the floods clap their hands, and let the hills be joyful together before the Lord; for he is come to judge the earth.

10 With righteousness shall he judge the world, and the people with equity.

After the second lesson:

Psalm 103. Benedic anima mea.

PRAISE the Lord, O my soul; and all that is within me, praise his holy Name.

2 Praise the Lord, O my soul, and forget not all his benefits:

3 Who forgiveth all thy sin, and healeth all thine infirmities;

4 Who saved thy life from destruction, and crowneth thee with mercy and loving-kindness;

5 Who satisfieth thy mouth with good things, making thee young and lusty as an eagle.

6 The Lord executeth rightousness and judgment for all them that are oppressed with wrong.

7 He showed his ways unto Moses, his works unto the children of Israel.

8 The Lord is full of compassion and mercy, long-suffering and of great goodness.

9 He will not alway be chiding; neither keepeth he his anger for ever.

10 He lath not dealt with us after our sins; nor rewarded us according to our wickednesses.

11 For look how high the heaven is in comparison of the earth; so great is his mercy also toward them that fear him.

12 Look how wide also the east is from the west; so far hath he set our sins from us.

13 Yea, like as a father pitieth his own children; even so is the Lord merciful unto them that fear him.

14 For he knoweth whereof we are made; he remembereth that we are but dust.

15 The days of man are but as grass, for he flourisheth as a flower of the field.

16 For as soon as the wind goeth over it, it is gone; and the place thereof shall know it no more.

17 But the merciful goodness of the Lord endureth for ever and ever upon them that fear him; and his righteousness upon children's children;

18 Even upon such as keep his covenant, and think upon his commandments to do them.

19 The Lord hath prepared his seat in heaven, and his kingdom ruleth over all.

20 O praise the Lord, ye angels of his, ye that excel in strength; ye that fulfill his commandment, and hearken unto the voice of his word.

21 O praise the Lord, all ye his hosts; ye servants of his that do his pleasure.

22 O speak good of the Lord, all ye works of his in all places of his dominion: praise thou the Lord, O my soul.

A Collect for Peace.

O God, from whom all holy desires, all good counsels, and all just works do proceed: Give unto thy servants that peace, which the world cannot give; that our hearts may be set to obey thy commandments, and also that by thee, we, being defended from the fear of our enemies, may pass our time in rest and quietness; through the merits of Jesus Christ our Saviour. *Amen.*

A Collect for Aid against Perils.

O Lord, our heavenly Father, by whose Almighty power we have been preserved this day; By thy great mercy defend us from all perils and dangers of this night; for the love of thy only Son, our Saviour, Jesus Christ. *Amen.*

AFTERWORD

The materials following were not in the original; but are added for the reader's edification.

SPECIAL PRAYERS SET FORTH FOR USE BY BISHOP ATKINSON

In the winter of 1860-1.

ALMIGHTY God, our Heavenly Father, in Whose hands are the hearts of men and the issues of events, and Who hast graciously promised to hear the prayers of those who, in an humble spirit, and with true faith, call upon Thee; be pleased, we beseech Thee, favorably to look upon and bless the Governor of this Commonwealth, its General Assembly now in session, and the people over whom they are chosen to rule.

Possess their minds with the spirit of wisdom and sound understanding, so that, in these days of trouble and perplexity, they may be able to perceive the right path, and steadfastly to walk therein.

So enlighten, direct and strengthen them, we pray Thee, that they, being hindered neither by the fear of man, nor by the love of the praise of men, nor by malice, nor by ambition, nor by any other evil passion, but being mindful of Thy constant superintendence, of the awful Majesty of Thy righteousness and of the strict account they must hereafter give to Thee, may, in counsel, word and deed, aim supremely at the fulfillment of their duty, at the promotion of Thy glory, and the advancement of the welfare of our country.

And grant that the course of this world may be so peaceably ordered by Thy governance, that Thy Church, and this whole people, may joyfully serve Thee in all godly quietness, through Jesus Christ our Lord. Amen.

A prayer for those who have gone forth to war in defense of their State and Country.

O MOST Gracious Lord God, our Heavenly Father, we commend to Thy care and protection Thy servants, who in behalf of their families and their country have gone forth to meet the dangers of war.

Direct and lead them in safety; bless them in their efforts to protect and defend this land; preserve them from the violence of the sword and from sickness; from injurious accidents; from treachery and from surprise; from carelessness of duty, from confusion and fear; from mutiny and disorder, from evil living, and from forgetfulness of Thee.

Enable them to return in safety and honor; that we being defended from those who would do us hurt, may rejoice in thy mercies, and Thy Church give Thee thanks in Peace and Truth, through Jesus Christ our Lord. Amen.

A Prayer for the People of
THE CONFEDERATE STATES.

O LORD, our God, Who rulest over all the Hosts of Heaven, and over all the nations of the earth, Thou hast power to cast down, or to raise up whomsoever Thou wilt, and to save by many or by few; and we now come to Thee to help and defend us in this time of danger and necessity.

We acknowledge and lament, O God, the many grievous sins, by which we have justly provoked Thy wrath and indignation, and wert Thou extreme to mark iniquities, O Lord, we could not abide it. But it is Thy nature and property ever to have mercy and to forgive; and we beseech Thee now to extend to us Thine accustomed mercy, and to deliver us from the evils and dangers to which we are exposed.

Do Thou, O Lord, remove from our borders all invading armies; confound the devices of such as would do us hurt, and send us speedily a just and honorable and lasting peace. And above every earthly blessing give us, as a people, grace to know, and love, and serve Thee, through Jesus Christ our Lord. Amen.

PRAYERS REQUESTED BY PRESIDENT JEFFERSON DAVIS

A Prayer for The Confederate States

Almighty God, the Sovereign disposer of events, it hath pleased thee to protect and defend the **CONFEDERATE STATES**, hitherto in their conflict with their enemies, and be unto them a shield.

With grateful thanks we recognize thy hand, and acknowledge that not unto us, but unto Thee belongeth the victory, and in humble dependence upon thy Almighty strength, and trusting in the justness of our cause. We appeal to Thee, that it may please Thee to set at naught the efforts of all our enemies, and put them to confusion and shame.

O, Almighty God! we pray Thee, that it may please Thee, to grant us Thy blessing upon our arms, and give us victory over all our enemies wherever they may be; preserve our homes and Altars from pollution, and secure to us the restoration of peace and prosperity — all of which we ask in the name of JESUS CHRIST, our blessed Lord and Saviour—to whom with the Father and the Holy Spirit, we will give all the praise and glory in time and throughout all eternity! Amen.

A DAY OF FASTING & HUMILIATION 1861 by JEFFERSON DAVIS, PRESIDENT OF THE CONFEDERATE STATES

WHEREAS, it hath pleased almighty God, the Sovereign Disposer of events, to protect and defend us hitherto in our conflicts with our enemies as to be unto them a shield.

And whereas, with grateful thanks we recognize His hand and acknowledge that not unto us, but unto Him, belongeth the victory, and in humble dependence upon His almighty strength, and trusting in the justness of our purpose, we appeal to Him that He may set at naught the efforts of our enemies, and humble them to confusion and shame.

Now therefore, I, JEFFERSON DAVIS, President of THE CONFEDERATE STATES, in view of impending conflict, do hereby set apart Friday, the 15th day of November, as a day of national humiliation and prayer, and do hereby invite the reverend clergy and the people of these Confederate States to repair on that day to their homes and usual places of public worship, and to implore blessing of almighty God upon our people, that he may give us victory over our enemies, preserve our homes and altars from pollution, and secure to us the restoration of peace and prosperity.

Given under hand and seal of the Confederate States at Richmond, this the 31st day of October, year of our Lord, one thousand eight hundred and sixty one.

By the President, Jefferson Davis.

THANKSGIVING DAY 1862 for victory in battle

To the People of the CONFEDERATE STATES:

Once more upon the plains of Manassas have our armies been blessed by the Lord of Hosts with a triumph over our enemies. It is my privilege to invite you once more to His footstool, not now in the garb of fasting and sorrow, but with joy and gladness, to render thanks for the great mercies received at His hand. A few months since, and our enemies poured forth their invading legions upon our soil. They laid waste our fields, polluted our altars and violated the sanctity of our homes. Around our capital they gathered their forces, and with boastful threats, claimed it as already their prize. The brave troops which rallied to its defense have extinguished these vain hopes, and, under the guidance of the same almighty hand, have scattered our enemies and driven them back in dismay. Uniting these defeated forces and the various armies which had been ravaging our coasts with the army of invasion in Northern Virginia, our enemies have renewed their attempt to subjugate us at the very place where their first effort was defeated, and the vengeance of retributive justice has overtaken the entire host in a second and complete overthrow.

To this signal success accorded to our arms in the East has been graciously added another equally brilliant in the West. On the very day on which our forces were led to victory on the Plains of Manassas, in Virginia, the same Almighty arm assisted us to overcome our enemies at Richmond, in Kentucky. Thus, at one and the same time, have two great hostile armies been stricken down, and the wicked designs of their armies been set at naught.

In such circumstances, it is meet and right that, as a people, we should bow down in adoring thankfulness to that gracious God who has been our bulwark and defense, and to offer unto him the tribute of thanksgiving and praise. In his hand is the issue of all events, and to him should we, in an especial manner, ascribe the honor of this great deliverance.

Now, therefore, I, JEFFERSON DAVIS, President of THE CONFEDERATE STATES, do issue this, my proclamation, setting apart Thursday, the 18th day of September inst., as a day of prayer and thanksgiving to Almighty God for the great mercies vouchsafed to our people, and more especially for the triumph of our arms at Richmond and Manassas; and I do hereby invite the people of THE CONFEDERATE STATES to meet on that day at their respective places of public worship, and to unite in rendering thanks and praise to God for these great mercies, and to implore Him to conduct our country safely through the perils which surround us, to the final attainment of the blessings of peace and security.

Given under my hand and the seal of the Confederate States, at Richmond, this fourth day of September, A.D.1862.

JEFFERSON DAVIS

February 27, 1863: CALL FOR A DAY OF PRAYER

Proclamation by the President.

The Richmond Enquirer, of the 28th February., contains a proclamation of JEFF. DAVIS, appointing the 27th day of March as a day of fasting, humiliation and prayer.

It is meet that, as people who acknowledge the supremacy of the living God, we should be ever mindful of our dependence on Him, and should remember that to Him alone can we trust our deliverance, that to him is due the devout thankfulness for signal mercies bestowed on us, and that by prayer alone can we hope to receive continued manifestation of that protecting care which has hitherto shielded us in the midst of trials and dangers. In obedience to this precept, we have from time to time been gathered together with prayers and thanksgiving, and He has been graciously pleased to hear our supplications, and to grant abundant exhibitions of His favor to our arms and our people.

Through many conflicts we have now attained a place among nations which commands their respect, and let the enemies who encompass us around and seek our destruction see that the Lord of Hosts has again taught them the lesson of His inspired word, "that the battle is not to the strong," but to whomsoever He willeth to exalt. Again an enemy, with loud boasting of power, of their armed men and mailed ships, threaten us with subjugation, and with evil machinations seek, even in our homes and at our own firesides, to pervert our men servants and our maid servants into accomplices of their wicked designs.

Under these circumstances it is my privilege to invite you once more to meet together and prostrate yourselves in humble supplication to Him who has been our constant and never-failing support in the past, and to whose protection and guidance we trust for the future. To this end I, JEFFERSON DAVIS, President of the CONFEDERATE STATES OF AMERICA, do issue this, my proclamation, setting apart Friday, the 27th day of March, as a day of fasting, humiliation and prayer.

I do also invite the people of the said States to repair, on that day, to their usual places of public worship, there to join in prayer to Almighty God that he will continue his merciful protection over our cause; that he will scatter our enemies and set at naught their evil designs, and that he will graciously restore to our beloved country the blessings of peace and security.

In faith whereof I have hereunto set my hand, at the City of Richmond, on the 27th day of February, in the year of our Lord, 1863.

(Signed) JEFFERSON DAVIS.

By the President.

(Signed) J.P. BENJAMIN, Secretary of State.

March 7, 1863: CALL FOR A DAY OF PRAYER

Proclamation by the President.

It is meet that as a people who acknowledge the supremacy of the living God, we should be even mindful of our dependence on Him; should remember that to Him alone can we trust for our deliverance; that to Him is due devout thankfulness for the signal bestowed on us; and that by prayer alone can we hope to secure the continued manifestation of that protecting care which has hitherto shielded us in the midst of trials and dangers.

In obedience to His precepts we have from time to time been gathered together with prayers and thanksgiving and He has been graciously pleased to hear our supplications, and to grant abundant exhibition of favor to our armies and our people. Through many conflicts we have now attained a place among the nations which commands their respect; and to the enemies who encompass us around and seek our destruction the Lord of Hosts has again taught the lesson of His inspired word; That the battle is not to the strong, but to whomsoever He willeth to exalt.

Again our enemy, with loud boasting of the power of their armed and mailed ships threaten us with subjugation, and, with evil machinations, seek even in our own homes and at our own firesides, to pervert our men-servants and our maid-servants into accomplices of their wicked designs.

Under these circumstances it is my privilege to invite you once more to meet together and to prostrate yourselves in humble supplication to Him who has been our constant and never failing support in the past and to whose protection and guidance we trust for the future.

To this end I, JEFFERSON DAVIS, President of the CONFEDERATE STATES OF AMERICA, do issue this my proclamation, setting apart Friday, the 27th day of March, as a day of fasting, humiliation, and prayer, and I do invite the people of the said States to repair on that day to their usual places of public worship, and to join in prayer to Almighty God that he will continue His merciful protection over our cause, that He will scatter our enemies, and set at naught their evil designs and that He will graciously restore to our beloved country the blessings of peace and security.

In faith whereof I have hereunto set my hand at the city of Richmond on the twenty-seventh day of February, in the year of our Lord one thousand eight hundred and sixty three.

JEFFERSON DAVIS.

By the President,

J. P. BENJAMIN, Secretary of State.

A SERMON

PREACHED IN

CHRIST CHURCH, SAVANNAH,

On Friday, November 15th, 1861,

BEING THE DAY OF

HUMILIATION, FASTING, AND PRAYER,

APPOINTED BY

THE PRESIDENT OF THE CONFEDERATE STATES.

"But they that wait upon the Lord shall renew their strength."
- ISAIAH 40:31.

1861

To the Clergy of the Diocese of Georgia

The President of the Confederate States having issued his proclamation appointing Friday, Nov. 15th, as a Day of Fasting, Humiliation and Prayer, and inviting all the citizens of the Confederate States to unite on that day in imploring the blessings of Almighty God upon our arms, that He may give us victory over our enemies, and preserve our homes and altars from pollution, and secure to us the restoration of peace and prosperity —

Now, therefore, I, STEPHEN ELLIOTT, Bishop of the Protestant Episcopal Church in the Diocese of Georgia, do direct the clergy of said Diocese to assemble their congregations upon that day, and to keep the Fast in all humility of mind and spirit.

Upon the occasion of the Fast the clergy will use the following service:

Morning prayer as usual to the

Psalter. Psalms for the day—27th,

77th, 130th. 1st Lesson—Isaiah,

chapter XL. 2d Lesson—Romans,

chapter XII. Use the Lesser Litany,

Immediately before the General Thanks-giving introduce the confession which precedes the Epistle in the service for Ash Wednesday, and the following Prayer:

"O Lord God, that dwellest in the Heavens and who reignest over all the kingdoms of men, we praise and bless Thy name that, in our troubles and perils, Thou hast stood on our side and pleaded for us against them that rose up against us. It was Thy hand, O Lord, and the help of Thy mercy that relieved us. Thou, O Lord, didst blast the designs of our enemies with the breath of Thy displeasure, and to Thee we ascribe the praise and honor of our present safety. Perpetuate Thy mercies to us; let a guard of Holy Angels stand round about us and about all Thy people, like the hills, for our defense and safety, that we may be inaccessible by all the attempts of our enemies. Let us receive the blessings which our Lord Jesus Christ left unto His Church, even the peace of God the Father, God the Son, and God the Holy Ghost, to whom be all honor and glory, now and forever." Amen.

Given under my hand, this November 11th, A. D. 1861.

STEPHEN ELLIOTT,
Bishop of the Diocese of Georgia.

A Sermon

ISAIAH 40:31. — "But they that wait upon the Lord shall renew their strength; they shall mount up with wings as eagles; they shall run and not be weary; and they shall walk and not faint."

We are realizing more and more every day, my beloved hearers, that we are engaged in a conflict which will demand all our strength, and will severely try our fortitude.

We did not enter upon it without long forbearance, and earnest consideration We postponed the evil day from year to year, hoping that there might be some change in the national policy, or some remembrance of what was due from brethren to brethren.

Long years ago we were forced to calculate the value of the Union, but even when we had decided, that in an economical point of view, it was worth but little to us, we yet clung to it with feelings which rose above all calculation — feelings of reverence for the past, and of devotion to the cause of constitutional liberty.

Although our statesmen and especially He, whose understanding seemed to have been endowed by God with almost the grasp of a prophetic spirit, had warned us to prepare for the consequences which have now come upon us, we could but slowly bring ourselves to believe that such a glorious fabric of Government would be sacrificed upon the altars of avarice and fanaticism.

It was not until we clearly perceived that our choice lay between an armed contest for our liberties, and an inevitable destruction of the whole framework of our social life, that we determined to meet the steadily approaching danger, and to leave to our children the memory, at least, of our struggles, and of our sacrifices.

We counted the cost deliberately; we discussed for years the elements of power which would be found upon the one side and the other; we weighed in the balances of a severe judgment, the evils which threatened us on either hand, and with a full understanding of what was before us, of the deep solemnity of the act, of our responsibilities to God as well as to man, of the terrible struggle we should have to wage, of the sacrifices we should be called upon to endure — sacrifices of affection far more dreadful than those of interest — we committed ourselves to Him who ruleth righteously, and assumed our place among the nations of the earth.

This thing was not done hastily, nor in a corner; it should have come unexpectedly to no man. For twenty years have the feelings which have at last brought it about, been intensifying and the purposes maturing.

It could not have been prevented, save by such a miraculous intervention as God neither vouchsafes in these latter days, nor did the Union deserve. The evil day might have been postponed; but such postponement would have been fatal to us. When we saw clearly that it must be done, then our welfare consisted in its being quickly done.

But although quickly done, and decidedly done, it was the execution of an act long deliberated upon and well matured. The determination was as great upon the one side as the other — the determination of a majority to over-ride all constitutional barriers, in order to grasp permanent power — the determination of a minority to preserve its constitutional rights, or to perish in the attempt.

And this long deliberation, together with the mighty interests involved in this struggle, satisfies me that we are only at the beginning of a long and bloody conflict, and that it is the duty of every one to consider it so and to prepare himself for such a contingency. A hasty quarrel may easily be settled, but a quarrel which has been festering for a quarter of a century, must be fought out.

Passion is very different from hatred and malice; the one may be satisfied with a momentary struggle, the other will continue their work of evil until they have glutted their vengeance, or have been utterly defeated. I can see no room for hope of any early or decided settlement of this question.

National exhaustion, foreign interference, commercial necessities, none of them can be counted upon as successful mediators, They may become important elements in the question at some distant period, but not now.

We must first pass through what we have deliberately said, as a sovereign power, that we anticipated and as solemnly announced that we were prepared for. No new or strange thing has come upon us. The assertion of national rights against irresponsible power has always produced long wars, because the one party is striving to regain a prestige which it has lost, while the other is battling for right, for conscience, for its altars and its firesides.

The recollection of our revolutionary war should teach us what to expect in a struggle of this sort. Nothing was more foolish than the continuance of that war, nothing more hopeless than any successful issue for England, and yet, from wounded pride, from unwillingness to give up the brightest jewels of the British crown, it was protracted for seven long years. And so will it be with this; success will be alternate, but never decisive.

Hope will be buoyed up by partial victories, until at last, wearied and exhausted, peace will be wrung from our enemies through sheer necessity. But that is far off, and ere we reach that point, we shall have been disciplined by much sorrow and purified in the furnace of affliction.

It is, I have no doubt, from such a view of the question as this, that the wise Statesman, whom we have placed at the head of our affairs, has decided upon the defensive policy which he is pursuing. An ambitious man, or a rash man, would have adopted a more brilliant and dashing career, but would have risked every thing by his movements. Defeat would have been almost irretrievable, and even success would have exhausted us if bought with the sacrifice of our best blood. Wars must be conducted according to their purposes.

Wars of conquest, such as those of Alexander, or Caesar, or Napoleon, demand a perpetual advance from victory to victory, but wars maintained for national independence, must be, necessarily, defensive. The stronger party must be forced to break his power against the barriers of nature, or the entrenchments of art. Space had more to do with the final overthrow of Napoleon than all his enemies combined. And this was Washington's policy during our revolution, and Wellington's policy for the deliverance of Portugal and Spain. It is not a popular mode of warfare, but it is a wise one, and demands a high degree of moral courage to pursue and maintain.

And one of those sins for which we should humble ourselves before God this day, is the murmuring in which we have been indulging because we have been restrained from aggression, and a waste of human life.

Not satisfied with having maintained our whole ground — with having repulsed our enemies in successive battles — with having confines him, when he has been victorious, to islands and deserts — with having received from God the most signal manifestations of His presence and favor, we have been tempted to pursue the wretched policy of our enemies, and to force upon our Statesmen and Generals, a line of conduct which has been rejected by their mature judgment and superior knowledge of all the circumstances of the case.

What greater mortification could we have inflicted upon our enemy, than we have inflicted, by confining all his movements to a given line, and whipping him whenever he dared to cross it? What more depressing influence could we bring to bear upon the people of the Government against which we are contending, than the forced inactivity of their Generals and armies?

It is already producing its effect among them, and their constant change of commanding officers, proves their dissatisfaction and their restlessness. And we must do the same thing here and every where; confine our enemies to the narrowest possible limits, and force them to war against all the natural defenses of the country, as well as the artificial ones.

They will soon be tired of such a warfare, for they must carry it on at an enormous expense, liable to all the contingencies of the ocean, with nothing but a desert around them, while we shall be in the midst of all our resources, suffering only the inconveniences which may arise from the abandonment of a limited line of coast, and the interruption of our foreign commerce.

By this defensive policy, we equalize ourselves with our enemies, superior as they are in numbers and equipments. Our defenses neutralize their arms, and the preservation of our men from slaughter will give us very soon, under the strict discipline of the camps, an army of veterans along our whole line, which will be irresistible when it is called upon to move.

Our danger, in a contest with a population so much larger than our own, is that we shall have no reserve, if we too rapidly exhaust our men. But by caring for every man's life, by considering it a sacred trust given to the Republic, and not to be expended except for necessity sake, we shall have enough and more than enough of whole hearted and whole souled men to carry us successfully through the conflict.

Nothing is so disastrous to us, at this juncture, as the destruction of confidence, among the people, in those who have been set over us by our own deliberate choice. Let us, as a nation, repent this day of this sin; for the divisions of Reuben, let there be great searchings of heart; let us all learn a new lesson under this our new Government, and endeavor to regain a virtue almost lost in this western world—the virtue of reverence—and the lesson of respecting, obeying, and honoring authority, for authority's sake.

But besides this evil of discord which has lifted its head among us, and which we pray may be exorcised by this day's humiliation, we have been manifesting, as a consequence of our repeated victories, a spirit of presumption, which is very much akin to the sin of saying — "My power and the might of mine hand hath gotten me this victory."

Immediately after our great and signal victory at Manassas, God was in all our thoughts; we praised Him, we magnified Him, we glorified Him, we gave thanks to His most glorious Majesty for His wonderful inter-position in our behalf; but as time has rolled on, the arm of flesh has been gradually taking the place, in our language at least, if not in our thoughts, of the power of God.

We have been hearing, of late, a great deal more about the skill of our Generals, about the valor of our troops, about the cowardice of our foes, than about God as our shield and defense.

We have talked as if all that was necessary to victory, was that our troops should be let loose upon our enemies, and as if He, who ruleth in all the armies of the sky, had nothing to do with success or defeat.

No spirit can be more fatal to us than this, for while it is especially hateful to God, it is the very worst policy in the world to despise one's enemies. We should have proper confidence in ourselves; we should go into battle praying and trusting that we may be victorious, but the moment that we consider victory as necessarily chained to our chariot wheels, we are in imminent danger both from God and man — from God, because He will not have His glory given to another, and from man, "because pride goeth before destruction, and an haughty spirit before a fall."

If we cherish this vain glorious temper, God will assuredly lay His hand upon those very things of which we make our boast — will take away our brave and skilful commanders by the edge of the sword, or will set them at discord among themselves, or will render them incompetent in the field — will blow the breath of His anger upon our gallant soldiers, and fill them with a fear unknown to them before, because supernatural and divine.

He is jealous of his glory, and especially jealous when he has taken a people, with their rulers and armies, so manifestly under His own guidance, as he has this people. He is leading us by His own way to our independence and rest, and we must learn to feel, as well as to acknowledge, the song of thanksgiving which David sang before the Lord in the hour of his prosperity:

"Thine, O Lord, is the greatness, and the power, and the glory, and the victory, and the majesty; for all that is in the heaven and in the earth is thine; thine is the kingdom, O Lord, and thou art exalted as Head above all."

And what shall I say of those more private sins which are disfiguring the fair face of our great national structure, and which will bring destruction with them if they continue to increase, the sins of intemperance, of profaneness, of irreligion, of extortion.

In the first burst of enthusiasm, when with the most solemn feelings, we were entering upon this our great work, religion seemed to hold paramount sway. Every body turned to God in Christ as his refuge and help; every body was lifted above low vices by the sublimity of the cause, and the greatness of the work which he had undertaken to do. It was a glorious moral spectacle which these sovereign States presented, when in prayer and with fasting, they placed themselves in the hands of God and committed themselves to His keeping.

And cannot that state of things continue? Must God's blessing and goodness forever work ingratitude and irreligion? Must the very success he has vouchsafed us turn our heads and hearts, and deliver us over to ourselves again? Must the noble virtues of temperance, of sobriety, of self-denial, always die out with the necessities which have produced them?

Must the graces of prayer and of supplication be laid aside the moment that God has given us the victory and fulfilled our heart's desire? God forbid! Let us rise up to the height of this great argument, and put beneath our feet every thing that may lower and degrade it.

We are moving in the light of God's countenance, and the waving of His hand and the flashing of His eye are almost visible to us. And shall we, in such a presence, forget our dignity and the sublimity of our cause, and prove ourselves unworthy to be His agents and His instruments? No man should presume to touch this ark of our liberty with unhallowed hands and with unclean lips, and until he proves that he can control himself, should have no part nor lot in this great enterprise.

What we need in this sacred conflict, is deep earnestness, religious enthusiasm, a solemn sense of responsibility, a devotedness to the right and the true. The time is past for levity, for dissipation, for a trifling with God's holy name, for a disregard of sacred things. We have now entered upon work which demands all man's self-possession and woman's self-sacrifice, which will separate the wheat from the chaff, the pure gold from the worthless dross.

But there is a sin which should, more than all, humiliate us this day, and cause us to blush for very shame — the sin of Faithlessness.

God has rebuked us for it so lovingly in the last day or two by heaping new mercies upon us, and turning the silver lining of the cloud towards us, that we can only bow ourselves down to the dust in sadness, and confess our unworthiness of His care.

Alas for poor, weak human nature! How it is tied down to flesh and sense! How it trusts only in what it can see, and find support only in the visible and the perishable! Sad and perpetual memento of the fall, manifested under every religious dispensation, and clearly seen among ourselves at this very moment!

If a special Providence can be proved to a people, it has been proved to us; it has followed us in every step of our national life; it has been seen by land and by sea, in sunshine and in storm, upon the battle field and in the council chamber. We may strive to put it from us, but it comes in some new shape, more striking than the last, until proud unbelief is silenced, if not convinced.

And when these signal fires of His presence are lighted all around us, can we still doubt and distrust? Why so faithless, my beloved people? Why so unwilling to acknowledge God's presence and God's love? Why so loth to receive Him as Emmanuel — God with us?

Is it that you fear to think He is so near you, that you shrink from contact with so holy a Being? O ye of little Faith! When will you make God yours by reciprocating His love, and receiving Him as your very present help in every time of trouble?

Because of these sins, my beloved people, and the weakness which they have produced in the national life, our chief magistrate has exhorted us to wait upon the Lord, that we may renew our strength. Thanks be to God that he seems to know where a nation's weakness can be repaired, and that he leads his people to the altars of the church, and not to the broken cisterns of the world, for the renewal of their vigor.

Happy is the people that is in such a case; for they shall mount up with wings as eagles; they shall run and not be weary; and they shall walk and not faint." Man looks for a renewal of strength, in the increase of troops, in the arrival of arms, in the arrangement of defenses, and these, as secondary causes of victory, are of the very highest importance, but of what good are they all unless, at the same time, we wait upon the Lord, and supplicate Him to revive the Heart?

The value of troops, of arms, of fortifications, depends upon the courage of those who use them; upon the strength of Heart which is behind them — and that comes from God.

He can encourage, and He can make afraid! In His power are the hearts of the very bravest, and from Him do they derive their energy, their endurance, their fortitude, Many a man who does not pray himself, is sustained by the prayers of God's people, who are behind him, supplicating the Lord and crying for His help.

When the brave and youthful Joshua went out to battle against Amalek, Israel prevailed in the battle so long as Moses held up his hand toward God; but when he let down his hand, Amalek prevailed.

Let us believe, my beloved people, what is indicated by this scriptural example, and whenever we find our armies or ourselves fainting in spirit, or weary in sacrifice, let us lift up our hands afresh to the Lord and renew our strength at the throne of Grace.

"He giveth power to the faint: and to them that have no might he increaseth strength. Even the youths shall faint and be weary, and the young men shall utterly fall: but they that wait upon the Lord shall renew their strength; they shall mount up with wings as eagles; they shall run and not be weary; and they shall walk and not faint."

But not only is it for our armies that a constant renewal of strength will be required, but for the whole nation engaged in this solemn controversy.

As I said in the beginning of my sermon, we entered into this conflict after having counted the cost, and after repeated public declarations that we were ready to do and to suffer all things for the cause in which we were engaged.

But the sternness of reality is often very much beyond the anticipation or the expectation. And when, that reality first comes home to us, we are tempted to faint and grow weary, and to be despondent beyond the necessities of the occasion.

We imagine that our individual sufferings are the sufferings of the whole nation; that our personal sacrifices are felt alike by all, and that our cause is waning before the irresistible weight of power and resources.

But that is only, my beloved people, because our minds, or our imaginations, are filled with those things which are immediately about us, to the exclusion of other parts of the field, just as an object which is very near the eye absorbs the whole vision, and destroys for the time the ability to see beyond.

We are fainting and growing weary; our hearts are longing for the flesh pots of Egypt, for the times. when peace and quiet were around us, when trade and commerce flourished, when the golden harvest was gathered without hindrance or alarm.

Not, for a single moment, that any one of us would really prefer that inglorious condition of colonial vassalage to even the sternest severities of the conflict, but that the temptation intrudes itself upon the weakness of human nature, and upon the weariness of the body and the spirit.

Our support, my beloved people, in such moments, is in God; He must and He will renew our strength. "When my soul fainted within me," said Jonah, "I remembered the Lord: and my prayer came in unto thee, into thine holy Temple, for salvation is of the Lord."

And, surely, if in answer to our prayers, God did no more than bring back to our remembrance all His mercies of old, they would be enough to give us confidence in the darkest hour which might come upon us. A year has elapsed since we commenced this conflict — commenced it in uncertainty, in weakness, without union, seemingly without the means of carrying it on for any long period of time.

Compare our condition now, and see whether there is anything in the aspect of affairs to cause your hearts to faint.

What progress has the enemy made? He has taken one post upon the barren sands of the Atlantic, which the winds and the waves are forcing him to abandon, and with a mighty armament — the largest, perhaps, of the century — fitted out at an enormous expense, he is preparing to ravage our coasts. He cannot advance into the interior unless we cease to pray to God, and thus permit our hearts to faint within us, and our strength to fail.

Meanwhile we are fighting and conquering in the enemy's country, at least upon debatable land, and are driving him back whenever and wherever he advances. We have an abundance of food. God is dropping arms into our hands, as if from the skies, and our finances are not disordered. Every foreign enterprise which we have undertaken has succeeded, and Europe is fast getting to sympathize with us in our conflict.

If, under these circumstances, we faint or grow weary, we shall not be worthy of our ancestry. It is time to talk of such things when, like Washington, we shall be reduced to a handful of soldiers, treading the snows barefoot, half-clad, without arms, without powder, and retreating, almost the last hope of our liberties, before a victorious army; or, like Marion, are driven to the swamps to feed upon the roots of the earth.

We seem to forget, at times, that we are a mighty nation, organized, equipped, with our armies in the field, and our manufactories at work, dependent upon nobody for our success, but upon God! We are stronger this day than the enemy is — stronger in our union, in the skill of our generals, in the determination of our troops, in the cause in which we are engaged. We are stronger in the permanence of our resources, and in our ability to carry on a protracted warfare.

All we require, is a constant renewal of our strength through Faith, and a looking towards God; is such a spiritual intercourse with Him as shall keep Him on our side, for truly is He our strength and our salvation. "If God be for us, who can be against us?"

And that He is for us, He tells us every day — tells us so plainly that unless we believe him, we must count him a liar. And if for us now, why should He turn against us? He will turn against us only if we forsake or neglect Him — only if we are presumptuous enough to say, "My hand and the might of my power," — only if we put our trust in man, or in the son of man, and forget the Lord our God — only if we drive Him from our camps, by those sins which He abhors.

While our officers are training their men in discipline, in arms, in movement, if they would also impress upon them the great necessity of a high moral tone, we should soon be beyond all danger from our enemies. It is a great mistake to neglect moral power, while we are cultivating physical power; to forget all that strength which is derived from God and His spirit, the strength which comes from prayer, from sobriety, from godliness, from holiness.

It was those things which made the armies of Cromwell irresistible; which enabled the apprentices of London and the artisans of the towns to overcome the disciplined royalists, and the cavaliers of Prince Rupert. Could I but see a high moral tone pervading our armies, descending from the officers to the men, I should be satisfied.

But if it becomes fashionable, in the army or the navy, to despise religion, to confound it with hypocrisy, or with weakness, our strength will be gone; for in this conflict it will need constant renewal, and the way to renew it is to wait upon the Lord.

Believe me, my beloved hearers, that one day of fasting and prayer is worth more to us than a hundred ship loads of arms, if it be kept in spirit and in truth — that one day of earnest humiliation will give us more strength than any reinforcements.

Man may grow weary, but God never. "Fast thou not known; hast thou not heard, that the everlasting God, the Lord, the Creator of the ends of the earth, fainteth not, neither is weary?"

"Even the youths shall faint and be weary, and the young men shall utterly falls but they that wait upon the Lord shall renew their strength; they shall mount up with wings as eagles; they shall run and not be weary; and they shall walk and not faint."[2]

---

[2] For more sermons from the Confederate States, see "Sermons of the Confederacy," by Dr. William G. Peters, published by C.S. Publishing Office.

Various Books Published By

CONFEDERATE STATES PRINTING OFFICE3

You can find these fine books and others by C.S. Publishing Office at your favorite Bookseller, or at www.lulu.com

The Confederate States of America in Prophecy, by Rev. W.H. Seat, a Southern Methodist Minister, and is edited by Dr. William G. Peters. This work examines Daniel's prophecy of the of the Five Governments; with the United States as the Fifth Government and the Confederate States as the little stone cut from the mountain, as a revived Government of Judah.

The Eschatology of the United States as Restored Israel, and the Confederate States as a Restored Judah, is a secular prophecy of the people of North America as God's special chosen people.

In the heady days of Southern victories over Northern armies, Rev. Seat posits the future history of the Confederate States based upon the Prophet Daniel.

Sermons of the Confederacy 1861-1862, edited by Dr. William G. Peters, is a collection of sermons by Southern ministers, bishops, and priests, from 1861-1862.

These ministers cover, in their sermons and discourses, a wide range of subjects, from the cause of the War, differences between Yankees and Southerners, Negroes and their purpose among Southerners, the life and death of Confederate heroes, service to God, military service and Christian Faith, etc.

This is an excellent book for those who want to understand our Confederate ancestors, the C.S.A., and the South's Faith in God and victory in the face of implacable Northern invasion.

Sermons of the Confederacy 1863-1865, edited by Dr. William G. Peters, is a collection of sermons by Southern ministers, bishops, priests, and rabbi from 1863-1865, and a continuation from "Sermons of the Confederacy 1861-1862."

These men of God cover a wide range of subjects, from the cause of the War, differences between Yankees and Southerners, Negroes and their purpose among Southerners, the life and death of Confederate heroes, service to God, military service and Christian Faith, etc.

---

[3] Also designated as C.S. Printing Office. A division of Confederate States of America, Inc.

This is an excellent book for those who want to understand our Confederate ancestors, the C.S.A., and the South's Faith in God and victory in the face of death and destruction from Federal invasion.

The True Church Indicated to the Inquirer, by Bishop John McGill. Confederate Bishop of Richmond, Virginia, edited by Dr. William G. Peters.

Bp. McGill examines the claims of various and sundry groups to be the true Church. He examines these claims in the light of scripture, history, tradition and reason. Then he contrasts them against the claims of the Catholic Church to be the One, True Church, showing how the claims of all other groups fall short.

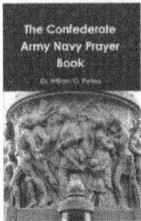

The Confederate Army Navy Prayer Book is the Episcopal Prayer Book for the Armed Services of the Confederacy, edited by Dr. William G. Peters. The Prayer Book went through annual editions from 1861-1865, and was the official military prayer book of the Confederate States.

Additional prayers have been included, including national calls to prayer by President Jefferson Davis throughout the War, and a sermon by Bp. Stephen Elliot delivered upon the Day of National Humiliation, Fasting and Prayer in 1861.

The Catholic Devotional for Confederate Soldiers was written by Bishop McGill for the Confederate soldiers to carry with them into battle, and for their encampments.

The work was published and registered by Bp. McGill in the Confederate States of America in 1861, and is edited by Dr. William G. Peters.

The Devotional contains many Catholic prayers, novenas, selections from the Mass, etc., which are appropriate to daily devotions, for Catholics and other Christians.

Faith The Victory by Bishop John McGill, Confederate Bishop of Richmond, Virginia, edited by Dr. William G. Peters.

Bp. McGill presents an explanation of Catholic doctrine for Catholics and non-Catholics who hold to the old orthodox Protestant beliefs and traditions, and want to know more about the development and meaning of Christian doctrine.

A non-polemical work, the Bishop provides a rational explanation of sometimes difficult subjects. It is a clear concise summary of doctrinal points of interest to all Christians, without being either too brief, or tedious.

www.ingramcontent.com/pod-product-compliance
Lightning Source LLC
Chambersburg PA
CBHW051813040426
42446CB00007B/653